THAI Dictionary & Phrasebook

THAI Dictionary & Phrasebook

THAI-ENGLISH
ENGLISH-THAI

Revised Edition

James Higbie

Hippocrene Books, Inc.
New York

For information, address:
HIPPOCRENE BOOKS, INC.
171 Madison Avenue
New York, NY 10016
www.hippocrenebooks.com

Library of Congress Cataloging-in-Publication Data

Higbie, James.
 Thai-English/English-Thai dictionary & phrasebook /
James Higbie. -- Rev.ed.
     p. cm.
 ISBN-13: 978-0-7818-1285-6 (pbk.)
 ISBN-10: 0-7818-1285-2 (pbk.)
1. Thai language--Dictionaries--English. 2. English
language--Dictionaries--Thai. 3. Thai language--
Conversation and phrasebooks--English. I. Title. II.
Title: Thai-English/English-Thai dictionary and
phrasebook.
 PL4187.H54 2012
 495.9'1321--dc23

                                        2012025472

CONTENTS

INTRODUCTION

Many people who visit or work in Thailand learn to speak Thai. This is partly from necessity, as few Thais speak English, but also because of some attractions of the Thai culture. In Thailand it is customary to talk to strangers. People will start talking to you everywhere you go, and will always be happy if you try to speak their language. The Thai language itself is easy and, with some effort to learn the basics, you can start having conversations with people right away.

Thai belongs to the Tai language family, a group of related languages spoken in Thailand, Laos, Burma (by the Shan ethnic group), northern Vietnam and southern China (by minority ethnic groups). The dialect spoken in Bangkok and surrounding areas is called Central Thai. It's the official language of Thailand and the language in this book. There are three other main Tai languages spoken in Thailand: Southern Thai, Northern Thai, and Northeastern Thai or Laotian, called *Ee-san* in Thailand. There are also local varieties of each language. These Tai dialects differ from each other mainly by vocabulary and are not mutually intelligible. It would take a person from Bangkok some time to be able to speak Northern Thai or another member of the Tai language family well.

Central Thai is the language of government, media, and education and is spoken throughout the country. People outside of central Thailand usually use their local languages at home but switch to Central Thai when they're in school or doing business. The many smaller ethnic groups who live in Thailand also learn to speak and read Central Thai in school.

Thai, like Vietnamese and the Chinese languages, is a tonal language. Learning to use the tones isn't easy and you need a good memory in order to remember both the letter pronunciation and the tone of every word. People often cut corners by ignoring the tones. This isn't a problem at first because Thai people won't expect perfect pronunciation from a beginner and will usually be able to figure out what you're trying to say. However, if you want to speak Thai well, you should learn the tones, and some words definitely need their tones to be understood, such as "five" (*ha*) which has a falling tone and "pork" (*moo*) which has a rising tone.

Thai words usually have only one syllable. The multi-syllable words in the language usually concern government, academic subjects, or religion and came to Thai through Sanskrit, a classical Indian language. You may notice a similarity between some high-level Thai words and equivalent English words. This arose through a historical connection between Greek and Latin and the ancient languages of central Asia and India. Many words are also borrowed from English.

The written form of Thai was also taken from Sanskrit. It's read phonetically from left to right like English but has more letters than English, for example there are four different letters for "s". Unlike English, the spelling of a word in Thai usually reflects its exact pronunciation and learning to read can help your pronunciation.

As you learn Thai you'll see how concise a language it is. English is often praised for its large vocabulary. Thai is the opposite, with a minimum of basic words and prefixes that are combined to form more complex meanings. The sentence structure is also simple, following the meaning of the sentence word by word. Thai does have grammar but it's a grammar of word order, not of changes in word form for tense or position.

Thai, like all languages, has variations in degree of correctness and formality. "R", for example, is almost always pronounced "l" informally but on

TV, in Thai language classes, and in polite situations people will try to pronounce "r" correctly. Vocabulary can also change and there are formal and informal variations for "eat", "drink", and many other words. As in English, people tend to use high-level vocabulary and more complicated sentence structure in formal situations.

One aspect of Thai culture evident from the language is an emphasis on politeness. Using polite forms of language in Thai shouldn't be thought of as demeaning to the speaker. In its best form the politeness in Thai reflects mutual respect, not a hierarchical social structure. Conversations in Thailand tend to be pleasant and fun. Controversial subjects aren't brought up and people usually don't speak sarcastically or abusively. In fact, talking loudly or rudely is taken seriously in Thailand and should be avoided.

Westerners usually find the spontaneous, relaxed atmosphere of the country very appealing and this is another reason why many people learn to speak Thai. It's an enjoyable place to travel and live in, and Thai people are so friendly you want to be able to talk to everyone you meet.

PRONUNCIATION

The system used here to write Thai words in the English alphabet maintains general English pronunciation, but there are four main points you should be aware of before starting to say Thai words. First, the letter *a* is pronounced "ah" as in "father," so the word for "house," *ban,* is pronounced "bahn." Secondly words with "o" such as *rot* ("vehicle") are pronounced with a long "o"— "rote." Another example is *mot* meaning "used up/all gone" which is pronounced "mote." Next, *ph* isn't pronounced "f" as in English but "p," and finally *th* is pronounced "t" not as "th" as in English. The single letters *t* and *p* are used to represent hard consonant sounds that aren't common in English.

Tones and vowel length
People learning Thai often feel that the pronunciation is one of the hardest things about the language. Thai is a tonal languge and has five distinct tones which are as much a part of a word's pronunciation as its letter sounds. Pronunciation in Thai varies not only by tone but by the length of the vowel sound. Thai words have either a long vowel length, with the pronunciation drawn out, or a short vowel length with the word pronounced quickly. In this book short vowel-length words are marked with an asterisk.

In all, there can be ten different pronunciations for every "word": the five tones each with two vowel lengths (although no Thai "word" has meanings for all ten). Try to listen to a Thai speaker pronounce these examples.

mid tone: Your normal speaking voice.

mid-short	yang	ยัง	still/yet
mid-long	yang	ยาง	rubber

low tone: Lower than your normal sound.

low-short	gae	แกะ	sheep
low-long	gae	แก่	old

falling tone: Start high and go down to a normal, mid sound.

falling-short	kao	เข้า	to enter
falling-long	kao	ข้าว	rice

high tone: Higher than your normal voice.

high-short	mai	มั้ย	interrogative
high-long	mai	ไม้	wood

rising tone: Start low and go up to a mid tone.

rising-short	laiŋ	ไหล	to flow
rising-long	laiŋ	หลาย	a lot

Consonants

Two consonant sounds may be difficult for English speakers. These are the **hard t** and **hard p**. The first is a cross between "t" and "d" like the "t" in "sixty," and the second is a cross between "p" and "b." Following is a list of consonant letters whose sounds are different from those in English:

g	has a hard sound, between "g" and "k"
j	a harder sound than in English
ng	the same as in English but used at the beginning of words
p	a hard p/b sound
ph	pronounced as "p" in English
r	slightly rolled, although "r" is usually pronounced as "l" in colloquial Thai

t	a hard t/d sound
th	pronounced as "t" in English

Vowels

a	as in "father"
ai	as in "Thai"
aw	as in "saw"
ay	"ay" as in "say"; or "eh" as in "bet"
ae	as in "cat"
e	as in "met"
ee	as in "see"
eu	as in the American pronunciation of "good"
euh	as in the British pronunciation of "Bert"
i	as in "bit"
o	as in "coat"
oo	as in "boot"
u	as in "but"

Vowel combinations

These combine two or more vowel sounds into one smooth sound. Some of them aren't used in English.

ao	ah+oh, as in "how"
aeo	ae+oh
eo	ay+oh, as in "mayo"
eua	eu+uh
euay	eua+ay+ėe
euy	euh+ee
ia	ee+uh, as in "Mia"
io	ee+oh as in "Leo"
iu	ee+oo, as in "mew"
oi	aw+ee
oy	oh+ee, as in "Chloe"
ua	oo+uh, as in "Kalua"
ui	oo+ee, as in "Louie"
uay	oo+ay+ėe, this sound ends with a very short "ėe"

Colloquial pronunciation

Following are some characteristics of informal Thai pronunciation:

r as l: "R" is almost always pronounced as "l." You may hear "hotel" pronounced *long-laem* instead of *rong-raem* and "vehicle" pronounced *lot* ("lote") instead of *rot* ("rote").

r/l omitted: "R" or "l" is left out when it's the second sound. *Gra-pao* ("suitcase") becomes *ga-pao* and *pla* ("fish") is *pa*.

Final sound/first syllable: In words such as *kot-sa-na* ("advertisement") and *phan-ra-ya* ("wife") the "t" and "n" at the end of the first syllable aren't pronounced.

BASIC GRAMMAR

In Thailand it's important to speak politely. There are two words, *ka* for women and *krup* for men, that are put at the end of questions, responses and statements to make them sound more polite. *Ka* and *krup* are also used to answer "yes" politely. You should always include these words when talking with someone you don't know or who is older than you, but they can be also used with people your own age to be polite. *Krup* has a single pronunciation but *ka* has three different pronunciations depending on how it's used. In this and other sections of this book, examples are marked (*f*) if they have the pronoun for women and/or *ka*, and (*m*) if they have the pronoun for men and/or *krup*.

polite word (*men, all uses*)   ครับ [krup]

polite word (*women for emphasis*)   คะ [ka]

polite word (*women for questions*)   คะ [ka]

polite word (*women for responses,*   คะ [ka]
   statements)

Pronouns vary according to the formality of the occasion and the relationship of the speakers. The following are those most commonly used. Note that in Thai the same word is both "I" and "me", "she" and "her", etc. In these examples the informal pronunciation of two pronouns is used – *chan* and *kao* are both marked high/short rather than with a rising tone as in the formal pronunciation.

I, me (*men, general*)	ผม	[phom]
I, me (*women, informal*)	ฉัน	[chan]
you	คุณ	[koon]
he, she, they, him, her, them	เขา	[kao]
we, us	เรา	[rao]
it	มัน	[mun]

Phuak is a pluralizer that is included with "we" and "they" for formality, or to clarify or emphasize that the number is plural.

we, us	พวกเรา [phuak rao]
they, them	พวกเขา [phuak kao]

Other common pronouns include:

I (*for children, means "mouse"*)	หนู [noo]
I, you, he, she (*intimate*)	เธอ [theuh]
I (*for women, formal*)	ดิฉัน [dee-chan]

For the **possessive** put the pronoun or name of the owner after *kawng*.

my, mine (*for men*)	ของผม [kawng phom]
my, mine (*for women*)	ของฉัน [kawng chan]
his, hers, theirs	ของเขา [kawng kao]
John's	ของจอห์น [kawng John]
whose	ของใคร [kawng krai]

These phrases are put after the name of the object with *kawng* optional as in the first example. The possessive isn't needed in phrases like "my mother" as in the second sentence.

Where's John's house?
บ้านของจอห์นอยู่ที่ไหน
Ban (kawng) John yoo thee-nai?

I live with my mother. (*f*)
ฉันอยู่กับแม่
Chan yoo gap mae.

Relationship terms are commonly used in place of "you" and "I." People who aren't actually related can be addressed as "aunt," "uncle," "grandmother," etc. *Phee* and *nawng* may be used for "you" and "I" among people from the same generation, the first for those older and the second for those younger than the speaker. More formally *phee* and *koon* ("you") are put before peoples' first names to show respect. *Koon* before a colleague's first name is common in offices or on the phone. When the word is written in English it's usually spelled *khun*.

younger person	น้อง [nawng]
older person	พี่ [phee]
formal title	คุณ [koon]

"To be" isn't used with adjectives in Thai. Feelings or descriptive words are put right after the subject of the sentence, as in the first example. *Mai* (with a falling tone, short vowel length) is put before an adjective or verb to make it negative.

I'm hungry. (*m*)
ผมหิวข้าว
Phom hiu-kao.

I'm not well. (*f*)
ฉันไม่สบาย
Chan mai sa-bai.

Daeng is beautiful.
แดงสวย
Daeng suay.

Adjectives and proper names are put directly after nouns. There is no "a," "the," or plural form. All colors have the word *see* (meaning "color") before them.

a big room (*lit*., "room-big")
ห้องใหญ่
hawng yai

the Erawan Hotel
โรงแรมเอราวัณ
Rong-raem Ay-ra-wan

Thai person/people
คนไทย
kon Thai

a white shirt (*lit.*, "shirt-color-white")
เสื้อสีขาว
seua seej kaoj

"To be" is used to link nouns only. There are two words for "to be": *pen* and *keu*. The first is more common. *Keu* is used only to link two things that are exact equivalents and is optional, as in the third example. The negative is made with *mai chai*. *Pen* and *keu* aren't included in the negative.

He's Chinese.
เขาเป็นคนจีน
Kao pen kon Jeen.

She's not Japanese.
เขาไม่ใช่คนญี่ปุ่น
Kao mai chai kon Yee-poon.

This is French wine.
นี่ (คือ) เหล้าฝรั่งเศส
Nee (keu) lao Fa-rang-set.

This isn't French wine.
นี่ไม่ใช่เหล้าฝรั่งเศส
Nee mai chai lao Fa-rang-set.

Yes/no questions are formed by putting *mai* (high tone, short vowel length) at the end of statements. Simple questions aren't answered with "yes" or "no" but by repeating the adjective or verb for "yes" or by putting *mai* (falling/short) before the adjective or verb for "no." Pronouns "you," "I," and "it" aren't needed in informal conversation if it's understood what or whom you're referring to.

Are you hungry?

(คุณ) หิวข้าวมั้ย

(Koon) <u>hiw</u>-kao‾ mai‾?

> Yes. / No.
>
> **หิว / ไม่หิว**
>
> <u>Hiw</u>. / Mai‾ <u>hiw</u>.

Is it good?

ดีมั้ย

Dee mai‾?

> Yes. / No.
>
> **ดี / ไม่ดี**
>
> Dee. / Mai‾ dee.

Is it fun?

สนุกมั้ย

Sa-<u>nook</u> mai‾?

> Yes. / No.
>
> **สนุก / ไม่สนุก**
>
> Sa-<u>nook</u>. / Mai‾ sa-<u>nook</u>.

Following are other words and phrases used for "yes" and "no."

yes (*polite for men*)	**ครับ** [krup‾]
yes (*polite for women*)	**คะ** [ka‾]
Yes, that's right.	**ใช่** [chai‾]
No, that's not right.	**ไม่ใช่** [mai‾ chai‾]

Two other ways to form **yes/no questions** are to include *reu plao* ("or not") or *reuh* (inflected question) at the end. Note that "you" is omitted in the following examples.

Are you going or not?

ไปรึเปล่า

Pai‾ reu‾ <u>plao</u>?

Yes. / No.
ไป / ไม่ไป
Pai. / Mai pai.

You're going?
ไปเหรอ
Pai <u>reuh</u>?

You're not going?
ไม่ไปเหรอ
Mai pai <u>reuh</u>?

A final way to form questions is with *chai mai* as a tag question. These questions are answered with *chai* for "yes" and *mai chai* for "no."

You're American, aren't you.
คุณเป็นคนอเมริกาใช่มั้ย
Koon pen kon A-may-ree-ga, chai mai?

Yes.
ใช่
Chai.

No. I'm Canadian. (*m*)
ไม่ใช่ ผมเป็นคนแคนาดา
Mai chai. <u>Phom</u> pen kon Kae-na-da.

Following are examples of **statements, negatives, and questions** using adjectives and verbs. The first example includes *mak* for "very." In the last example *mee* ("to have") means "there is / there are."

Thai food is very delicious.
อาหารไทยอร่อยมาก
A-<u>han</u> Thai a-<u>roi</u> mak.

Is Thai food delicious?
อาหารไทยอร่อยมั้ย
A-<u>han</u> Thai a-<u>roi</u> mai?

Yes.
อร่อย
A-roi.

Do you like Thai food?
คุณชอบอาหารไทยมั้ย
Koon chawp a-hang Thai mai?

Yes. / No.
ชอบ / ไม่ชอบ
Chawp. / Mai chawp.

I like Thai food. (*m*)
ผมชอบอาหารไทย
Phom chawp a-hang Thai.

Are you going to Phuket?
คุณจะไปภูเก็ตมั้ย
Koon ja pai Phoo-get mai?

Yes. / No.
ไป / ไม่ไป
Pai. / Mai pai.

I'm not going to Phuket. (*f*)
ฉันไม่ไปภูเก็ต
Chan mai pai Phoo-get.

Do you have ice? / Is there ice?
มีน้ำแข็งมั้ย
Mee nam-kaeng mai?

Yes. / No.
มี / ไม่มี
Mee. / Mai mee.

I don't have ice. / There's no ice.
ไม่มีน้ำแข็ง
Mai mee nam-kaeng.

"This" and "that" (*nee* and *nan*) are put directly after nouns informally as in these examples. In formal or correct Thai the classifier for the noun is included. See the explanation for classifiers below.

This hotel is good.
โรงแรมนี้ดี
Rong-raem nee dee.

That hotel isn't good.
โรงแรมนั้นไม่ดี
Rong-raem nan mai dee.

Is this restaurant expensive?
ร้านอาหารนี้แพงมั้ย
Ran-a-han nee phaeng mai?

> Yes, it's expensive.
> **แพง**
> Phaeng.

Include *laeo* ("already") for an **action or state that is completed**.

That's enough.
พอแล้ว
Phaw laeo.

I'm full.
อิ่มแล้ว
Im laeo.

He/She has come already.
เขามาแล้ว
Kao ma laeo.

The water's gone/used-up.
น้ำหมดแล้ว
Nam mot laeo.

I'm finished. / It's finished.
เสร็จแล้ว
Sèt laeo.

Put *gwa* after adjectives for the **comparative** ("bigger") and *thee-soot* for the **superlative** ("the biggest").

Bangkok is bigger than Chiang Mai.
กรุงเทพฯใหญ่กว่าเชียงใหม่
Groong-thayp yai gwa Chiang Mai.

Ko Phi Phi is the most beautiful.
เกาะพีพีสวยที่สุด
Gaw Phee-Phee suay thee-soot.

Tenses aren't complicated. Verbs have one form which can refer to any time—past, present, or future. There are four words which may be included to emphasize or clarify the meaning. With the present continuous ("I'm eating") *gam-lang* before the verb emphasizes that the action is continuous while *yoo* after the verb shows that the state exists. For the future, *ja* is put before the verb, while for the negative in the past tense *dai* is put between *mai* ("not") and the verb.

I'm studying Thai. (*f*)
ฉันเรียนภาษาไทย
Chan rian pha-sa Thai.

(*to emphasize that the action is continuous*)
ฉันกำลังเรียนภาษาไทย
Chan gam-lang rian pha-sa Thai.

(*to emphasize that the state exists*)
ฉันเรียนภาษาไทยอยู่
Chan rian pha-sa Thai yoo.

I will go to Ayuthaya. (*m*)

ผมจะไปอยุธยา

Phom̥ ja pai A-yoot-tha-ya.

I'm not going to Korat. (*m*)

ผมไม่ไปโคราช

Phom̥ mai pai Ko-rat.

He went swimming.

เขาไปว่ายน้ำ

Kao pai wai-nam.

I didn't go to Ubon. (*m*)

ผมไม่ได้ไปอุบล

Phom̥ mai dai pai Oo-bon.

Questions and statements with **"yet"** and **"still"** are formed as follows:

Has John gone yet?

จอห์นไปรึยัง

John pai reu yang?

Yes. / No.

ไปแล้ว / ยัง

Pai laeo. / Yang.

John's gone already.

จอห์นไปแล้ว

John pai laeo.

John hasn't gone yet.

จอห์นยังไม่ได้ไป

John yang mai dai pai.

John isn't going yet.

จอห์นยังไม่ไป

John yang mai pai.

John's still at home.
จอห์นยังอยู่บ้าน
John yang yoo ban.

Sentences with **auxiliaries** are formed with the following words:

have ever	เคย	[keuy]
have to	ต้อง	[tawng]
like to	ชอบ	[chawp]
might	อาจจะ	[at ja]
want to	อยาก	[yak]

Have you ever gone to Hua Hin?
คุณเคยไปหัวหินมั้ย
Koon keuy pai Huay Hiny mai?

Yes. / No.
เคย / ไม่เคย
Keuy. / Mai keuy.

I've gone to Hua Hin. (*f*)
ฉันเคยไปหัวหิน
Chan keuy pai Huay Hiny.

I've never gone to Hua Hin. (*m*)
ผมไม่เคยไปหัวหิน
Phomy mai keuy pai Huay Hiny.

I have to go to the bank. (*f*)
ฉันต้องไปธนาคาร
Chan tawng pai tha-na-kan.

I like to listen to music. (*m*)
ผมชอบฟังเพลง
Phomy chawp fang phlayng.

I don't like to drink (liquor). (*f*)
ฉันไม่ชอบกินเหล้า
Chan mai chawp gin lao.

I might go to Chiang Rai. (*m*)
ผมอาจจะไปเชียงราย
Phom at ja pai Chiang Rai.

I want to go shopping. (*f*)
ฉันอยากไปซื้อของ
Chan yak pai seu kawng.

I don't want to go. (*m*)
ผมไม่อยากไป
Phom mai yak pai.

There are two words for "**can**"—*dai* and *pen*. *Dai* is used for any meaning of "can" (availability, permission, ability) while *pen* is used for ability only. *Pen* is commonly used to ask if someone is "able" to eat certain kinds of food. Both words are put at the end of the question or statement. There is also the word *wai*, used mostly in the negative, to say that you're physically unable to do something— *mai wai* (rising tone/short vowel length on *wai*).

Can you go?
(คุณ) ไปได้มั้ย
(Koon) pai dai mai?

Yes. / No.
ได้ / ไม่ได้
Dai. / Mai dai.

I can go. (*m*)
ผมไปได้
Phom pai dai.

I can't go. (*f*)
ฉันไปไม่ได้
Chan pai mai dai.

Can you eat Thai food?

(คุณ) กินอาหารไทยเป็นมั้ย

(Koon) gin a-<u>hang</u> Thai pen mai?

Yes. / No.

เป็น / ไม่เป็น

Pen. / Mai pen.

Classifiers are used with numbers, how many, this/that, which, each, and some other patterns. They are used together with the noun (with the classifier put after the noun), or in place of the noun. Following is a list of common classifiers:

boats	ลำ	[lum]
books	เล่ม	[lem]
bottles	ขวด	[kuat]
buildings	หลัง	[lang]
clothing	ตัว	[tua]
glasses of drinks	แก้ว	[gaeo]
objects in general	อัน	[un]
pairs of things	คู่	[koo]
people	คน	[kon]
pieces of things	ชิ้น	[chin]
places	ที่, แห่ง	[thee, haeng]
plates of food	จาน	[jan]
round objects	ลูก	[look]
sets of things	ชุด	[choot]
small objects	ใบ	[bai]
strands (noodles; necklaces)	เส้น	[sen]
trees, plants	ต้น	[ton]
vehicles	คัน	[kun]

The following examples show how classifiers are used in phrases and sentences.

one bottle of water
("*water-one-classifier*")
น้ำหนึ่งขวด
nam ne̱ung kuat

How many shirts did you buy?
("*you-buy-shirts-how many-classifier*")
คุณซื้อเสื้อกี่ตัว
Koon seu seua̱ gee tua?

I bought two shirts. (f)
("*I-buy-shirt-two-classifier*")
ฉันซื้อเสื้อสองตัว
Chan seu seua̱ sawngɉ tua.

Which shirt do you like?
("*you-like-shirt-classifier-which*")
คุณชอบเสื้อตัวไหน
Koon chawp̱ seua̱ tua na̱iɉ?

I like this shirt. (m)
("*I-like-shirt-classifier-this*")
ผมชอบเสื้อตัวนี้
Phomɉ chawp̱ seua̱ tua nee.

For **requests** put *chuay* ("help") at the beginning and *noi* ("a little") or *duay* ("also") at the end. *Ka* and *krup* can also be included at the end to be more polite. For "don't" use *ya* or *mai tawng* before the verb. The first sounds strong or harsh. The second means "you don't have to" and sounds less harsh. The particle *na* (pronounced high/short) is put at the end of requests with "don't." It's a common word in Thai that means "mind you," "isn't it?," or "OK?" Use *kaw* when asking permission to do an action as in the last sentence. There are two words for "please" but they aren't common in everyday conversation and are used mostly on written signs.

Please open the window.
ช่วยเปิดหน้าต่างหน่อย
Chuay peuht na-tang noi.

Don't open the door!
อย่าเปิดประตูนะ
Ya peuht pra-too, na.

You don't have to close the door.
ไม่ต้องปิดประตูนะ
Mai tawng pit pra-too, na.

May I take your picture?
ขอถ่ายรูปคุณได้มั้ย
Kaw) thai roop koon dai mai?

Common **prepositions** are as follows:

about (*concerned with*)	เกี่ยวกับ [gio-gap]
about (*the subject of*)	เรื่อง [reuang]
about (*think, dream*)	ถึง [theung)]
at	ที่ [thee]
at (*be at*)	อยู่, อยู่ที่ [yoo, yoo thee]
for (*someone*)	ให้, สำหรับ [hai, sam)-rap]
from	จาก [jak]
in	ใน [nai]
with	กับ [gap]

What field do you study?
เรียนเกี่ยวกับอะไร
Rian gio-gap a-rai?

What are you talking about?

คุณคุยเรื่องอะไร

Koon kui reuang a-rai?

I thought about you. / I missed you. (*m*)

ผมคิดถึงคุณ

Phom kit theung koon.

I stay at a hotel. (*f*)

ฉันพักที่โรงแรม

Chan phak thee rong-raem.

Noi is at home.

หน่อยอยู่ (ที่) บ้าน

Noi yoo (thee) ban.

Lek is in Chiang Mai.

เล็กอยู่ (ที่) เชียงใหม่

Lek yoo (thee) Chiang Mai.

This is for you.

อันนี้ให้คุณ / อันนี้สำหรับคุณ

Un nee hai koon. *or* Un nee sam-rap koon.

I bought it for you. (*f*)

ฉันซื้อให้คุณ

Chan seu hai koon.

He comes from Myanmar.

เขามาจากพม่า

Kao ma jak Pha-ma.

He/She is in the room.

เขาอยู่ในห้อง

Kao yoo nai hawng.

I came with my older brother. (*m*)

ผมมากับพี่ชาย

Phom ma gap phee-chai.

Common **conjunctions** are as follows:

and (*then*)	แล้ว, แล้วก็	[laeo, laeo gaw]
and (*with*)	กับ	[gap]
but	แต่	[tae]
if	ถ้า	[tha]
or	หรือ	[reuɯ]
that (*say, think*)	ว่า	[wa]
that, which, who	ที่	[thee]

I'm going shopping and then I'm going to eat. (*m*)

ผมจะไปซื้อของแล้ว (ก็) ไปกินข้าว

Phom ja pai seu kawng laeo (gaw) pai gin kao.

I'm going to Pattaya and Ko Chang. (*f*)

ฉันจะไปพัทยากับเกาะช้าง

Chan ja pai Phat-tha-ya gap Gaw Chang.

I'm going but he isn't. (*f*)

ฉันจะไปแต่เขาไม่ไป

Chan ja pai tae kao mai pai.

If I have time I'll go to Ko Tao. (*m*)

ถ้ามีเวลาผมจะไปเกาะเต่า

Tha mee way-la phom ja pai Gaw Tao.

Are you going to Chiang Mai or Chiang Rai?

คุณจะไปเชียงใหม่หรือเชียงราย

Koon ja pai Chiang Mai reuɯ Chiang Rai?

What did she say?

เขาพูดว่าอะไร

Kao phoot wa a-rai?

She said that she wasn't coming.

เขาพูดว่าเขาไม่มา

Kao phoot wa kao mai ma.

I think he's coming today. (*m*)

ผมคิดว่าเขาจะมาวันนี้

Phom kit wa kao ja ma wan-nee.

The shirt that you bought is very nice.

เสื้อที่คุณซื้อสวยมาก

Seua thee koon seu suay mak.

The person who works there is named Maeo.

คนที่ทำงานที่นั้นชื่อแมว

Kon thee tham-ngan thee-nan cheu Maeo.

THAI-ENGLISH
DICTIONARY

Note: *In Thai, nouns are the same whether singular or plural. Only the singular form is given in the English translation.*

A

<u>ab</u>-nam อาบน้ำ to bathe, to take a bath

a-<u>gat</u> อากาศ air, weather, atmosphere, climate

a-<u>han</u> อาหาร food

<u>an</u> อ่าน to read

a-na-<u>kot</u> อนาคต future, the future

an-ta-rai อันตราย dangerous

ao เอา to want, to take

a-rai อะไร what

a-<u>roi</u> อร่อย delicious

a-rom อารมณ์ mood, emotion

<u>at</u> ja (verb) อาจจะ might

a-thit อาทิตย์ week

<u>awk</u> ออก to go out, to put forth

ayng เอง oneself

a-yoo อายุ age

B

baeng แบงค์ banknote

<u>baep</u> แบบ type, kind, style

<u>ban</u> บ้าน house, home

<u>ban</u> <u>nawk</u> บ้านนอก countryside (*informal term*)

bang (classifier) บาง some

bang บ้าง some, somewhat

bang-thee บางที maybe, sometimes

<u>bawk</u> บอก to tell

baw-ree-gan บริการ service; to serve

baw-ree-<u>sat</u> บริษัท company, business

baw-ree-<u>soot</u> บริสุทธิ์ innocent, pure

<u>beua</u> เบื่อ bored, tired of

bin **บิล** bill (*in restaurant*)

bin **บิน** to fly

bon **บน** on, on top of, above

bon **บ่น** to complain

bo-ran **โบราณ** ancient, antique; traditional

CH

cha **ช้า** slow, slowly; late

chai **ใช่** yes, that's right

chai **ใช้** to use

chai-daen **ชายแดน** border

cha-lat **ฉลาด** intelligent

chan **ฉัน** I, me (*for women, informal*)

chan **ชั้น** class, level, grade

chang **ช้าง** elephant

chao **ชาว** inhabitant of

chao **เช่า** to rent

chat **ชาติ** nation; nationality

chat **ชัด** clear, clearly

chawp **ชอบ** to like, to like to

cheu **ชื่อ** name, first name

cheua **เชื่อ** to believe

cheuy-cheuy **เฉยๆ** indifferent, impassive

chin **ชิน** accustomed to

chin **ชิ้น** piece

chok **โชค** luck

chok **ชก** to hit, to punch, to box

chon **ชน** to bump, to crash into

chon-na-bot **ชนบท** countryside

choot **ชุด** set, suit, uniform

chuan **ชวน** to invite

chuang **ช่วง** period, duration

chuay **ช่วย** to help

D

dai ได้ can, able to, to get

dai rap ได้รับ to receive

dai yin ได้ยิน to hear

dam, seej dam ดำ, สีดำ black

dang ดัง loud; famous

dao ดาว star; planet

dawk-mai ดอกไม้ flower

dee ดี good

dee gwa ดีกว่า better, would be better; would rather

dee-jai ดีใจ happy, glad

dee keun ดีขึ้น improved, better

dee thee-soot ดีที่สุด the best

dek เด็ก child, young person

deuan เดือน month

deuhn เดิน to walk

deuhn-thang เดินทาง to travel

deuk ดึก late (at night)

deum ดื่ม to drink

din ดิน soil

dio เดียว single, sole, only

dio-gan เดียวกัน one and the same

dioj เดี๋ยว in a moment

dioj-nee เดี๋ยวนี้ right now

don-tree ดนตรี music

doo ดู to look, to look at

doo meuanj ดูเหมือน to look like, to seem like

doo nangj ดูหนัง to see a movie

duan ด่วน express, urgent

duay ด้วย also, too

duay-gan ด้วยกัน together

E

eeg อีก more, again, in addition
eun อื่น other, some other

F

fa ฟ้า sky
faen แฟน boyfriend, girlfriend; husband, wife
fai ไฟ fire; electricity
fak ฝาก to deposit, to entrust
fang ฟัง to listen, to listen to
fao เฝ้า to guard, to watch over
feuk ฝึก to train, to practice
fonj ฝน rain
foon ฝุ่น dust
fun ฟัน tooth
fun ฝัน to dream

G

gae แก่ old (*for living things*); dark (*colors*);
  strong (*coffee, tea*)
gae แก้ to correct, to solve, to remedy
gaeo แก้ว drinking glass, crystal
gam-lang กำลัง power, force, energy
gam-lang-jai กำลังใจ will power, spirit
gan กัน each other (*follows verb*)
gan การ affairs of, matters of (*prefix*)
gan-meuang การเมือง politics
gao เก่า old (*for objects*)
gao เก้า nine
gap กับ with, and
gaw เกาะ island
gaw sang ก่อสร้าง construction work

gaw **ก็** still, also, subsequently (*linking word, hypothetical*)

gaw dai **ก็ได้** would be alright

gawn **ก่อน** first, before something else

gee (*classifier*) **กี่** how many

gee-la **กีฬา** sports

geng **เก่ง** expertly, well, good at

gep **เก็บ** to collect, to pick up, to keep

gep wai **เก็บไว้** to keep, to save

geuap **เกือบ** almost, nearly

geuhn pai **เกินไป** too (*as in* "too hot")

geuht **เกิด** to be born, to happen, to originate

gin **กิน** to eat, to drink (*informal*)

gin lao **กินเหล้า** to drink liquor

gin ya **กินยา** to take medicine

gio-gap **เกี่ยวกับ** about, concerning

glai **ไกล** far

glai **ใกล้** near

glang **กลาง** center, middle, central

glap **กลับ** to go back, to return, to turn back

glap ban **กลับบ้าน** to go home

glap ma **กลับมา** to come back

glap pai **กลับไป** to go back

glawng **กลอง** drum

glawng **กล่อง** box, carton

glawng thai roop **กล้องถ่ายรูป** camera

gliat **เกลียด** to hate

gloom **กลุ่ม** group (of people)

glua **กลัว** afraid

go-hok **โกหก** to lie, to tell a lie

gong **โกง** to cheat

goon-jae **กุญแจ** key; wrench (*tool*)

gra-dat **กระดาษ** paper

gra-jok กระจก window glass, mirror
gra-pao กระเป๋า suitcase, purse, pocket
gra-pawng กระป๋อง can (tin can)
gwa กว่า more than

H

ha ห้า five
ha หา to look for
haeng แห้ง dry
hai ให้ to give; to let, to allow
hai หาย gone, disappeared, missing
hak หัก to break (in two)
ham ห้าม don't (*forbidden*), to prohibit
hawm หอม good-smelling; to kiss
hawng ห้อง room
hen เห็น to see
hiu หิ้ว to carry (something with a handle)
hiu หิว hungry
hok หก six
hua หัว head
huay ห้วย stream
huay หวย lottery

I

im อิ่ม full (*from eating*)

J

ja จะ will, would
jai ใจ heart, mind (*figurative*)
jai-dee ใจดี glad, happy
jai-rawn ใจร้อน hot-tempered, impulsive, anxious
jai จ่าย to pay
jak จาก from; to go away from

jam จำ to remember

jam-gat จำกัด to limit, limited

jam-nuan จำนวน quantity, amount

jam-pen จำเป็น must, to be necessary

jang จั๊ง very, extremely

jang จ้าง to hire

jao kawng เจ้าของ owner (of)

jap จับ to touch; to catch, to arrest, to hold

jat จัด to arrange, to put in order, to prepare

jat จัด intense, strong

jawng จอง to reserve (rooms/seats)

jawng จ้อง to stare (at)

jawt จอด to park, to stop (a vehicle)

jeep จีบ to flirt with, to woo

jep เจ็บ to hurt, to be injured

jet เจ็ด seven

jeuh เจอ to meet, to run into unexpectedly, to find

jeut จืด bland, unseasoned

jing จริง true, real

jing-jai จริงใจ sincere

jon จน poor

jon จน until, up to the point of/that

jon โจร thief

joop จูบ to kiss

joot จุด point, spot, decimal point, period

joot จุด to ignite, to light (a fire)

jop จบ to finish, to end (an action of defined
    duration)

jot-mai จดหมาย letter

K

ka ข่า galangal (*type of ginger*)

ka ฆ่า to kill

kaî **ค่า** charge for, fee

kaî chaò **ค่าเช่า** rental fee

kaʲ **ขา** leg

kaî kaiʲ **ค่าขาย** to sell, to engage in trade

kaé **แค่** only (a small amount); to the extent of; level

kaek **แขก** guest

kaeng, kaeng-kuʲ **แข่ง, แข่งขัน** to race, to compete

kaeŋʲ **แข็ง** hard (*opp. of soft*)

kaeŋʲ-raeng **แข็งแรง** strong (*physically*)

kai **ไข่** egg

kaî **ไข้** fever

kaiʲ **ขาย** to sell

kam **คำ** word

kam, tawn kam **ค่ำ, ตอนค่ำ** evening

kam **ข้าม** to cross, to go across

ka-moy **ขโมย** to steal

ka-nat **ขนาด** size, extent, magnitude

kang **ข้าง** side, beside

kang keun **ค้างคืน** to stay overnight

ka-nomʲ **ขนม** snack, dessert

kao **ข่าว** news

kaò **เข้า** to enter, to go in

kaò-jaị **เข้าใจ** to understand

kaô **ข้าว** rice

kao **เขา** he, she, they

kaoʲ, seeʲ kaoʲ **ขาว, สีขาว** white

kap **ขับ** to drive

kat **ขาด** to tear; torn

kat **ขาด** to lack, to miss, missing

kaw **คอ** neck, throat

kaw ข้อ joint; node; point (*on a list*); *prefix for worded content*

kaw-moon ข้อมูล information

kawɟ ขอ to ask for, to request, to beg

kawɟ-thot ขอโทษ excuse me, to apologize

kawngɟ ของ thing, object, possession(s)

kawngɟ-kwanɟ ของขวัญ present, gift

kee ขี่ to ride

kee ขี้ excrement

kee ขี้ characterized by (*prefix for describing people*)

kee ai ขี้อาย shy

kem เค็ม salt, salty, salted

kemɟ เข็ม needle

keu คือ to be, that is to say

keun คืน to return (something borrowed)

keun ขึ้น up, to go up, to rise, to increase

keun-nee คืนนี้ this evening, tonight

keuy เคย have ever; used to

kianɟ เขียน to write, to draw

kit คิด to think, to calculate

klai คล้าย similar to

klawng คลอง canal

koi คอย to wait, to wait for

koi คอย gradually; gently

kom คม sharp

komɟ bitter

kon คน person, people; *classifier for people*

koo คู่ pair

koom ka คุ้มค่า to be worthwhile, to be worth it

koon คุณ you; value, virtue

koon-na-phap คุณภาพ quality

kop คบ to be friends

kot-sa-na **โฆษณา** advertisement; to advertise

krai **ใคร** who, anyone, whoever

krang **ครั้ง** time, occasion

kreuang **เครื่อง** machine, instrument, apparatus

kreung **ครึ่ง** half

krop **ครบ** complete, everything is there (that should be)

kuan ja **ควรจะ** should

kui **คุย** to talk, to converse

kun **คัน** itch; itchy

kun **คัน** *classifier for vehicles*

kwaj **ขวา** right (side)

kwam **ความ** *prefix used to form nouns*

kwam-maij **ความหมาย** meaning

kwam-rak **ความรัก** love (*n*)

kwam-reo **ความเร็ว** speed

kwam-sook **ความสุข** happiness

L

la awk **ลาออก** to quit (a job)

la **ละ** each, per

lae **และ** and (*formal, written*)

laeo **แล้ว** already, then

laeo gaw **แล้วก็** then

laeo tae **แล้วแต่** depends on, up to

laij (*classifier*) **หลาย** a lot, many

lam-bak **ลำบาก** a bother, difficult

lang **ล่าง** below, under

lang **ล้าง** to wash

langj **หลัง** *classifier for buildings*

langj **หลัง** back, behind

langj-jak **หลังจาก** after

lao **เหล้า** liquor

lap **หลับ** to sleep, to be asleep

law **หล่อ** handsome

law **ล้อ** wheel

lawng **ลอง** to try, to test out

lawt **หลอด** tube, drinking straw

lek **เล็ก** little (in size)

lem **เล่ม** volume; *classifier for books and carts*

len **เล่น** to play, to do something without a
serious purpose

leuhk **เลิก** to quit, to stop

leum **ลืม** to forget

leuy **เลย** completely, utterly; past a place;
therefore

liang **เลี้ยง** to pay for, to feed, to raise (children,
animals)

lio **เลี้ยว** to turn (a corner)

lo **โล** kilogram

lo **โหล** dozen

lok **โลก** the world, the earth

lom **ลม** wind (*n*)

lom **ล้ม** to fall over

long **ลง** to go down, to descend

look **ลูก** child (of one's own); *classifier for ball-
shaped objects*

look keun **ลูกขึ้น** to stand up, to get up

loong **ลุง** uncle

lot **ลด** to reduce, to decrease

luang **หลวง** official, royal

M

ma **มา** to come

ma **ม้า** horse

ma **หมา** dog

mae แม่ mother
mae-nam แม่น้ำ river
mai ใหม่ new, again (anew, newly)
mai ไหม้ to burn (is burning)
mai ไม่ no, not (*negative*)
mai keuy ไม่เคย have never
mai koi ไม่ค่อย not very
mai mee ไม่มี don't have, there isn't
mai meuan ไม่เหมือน different, not the same
mai มั้ย interrogative (*used to form questions*)
mai ไม้ wood
mai, pha mai ไหม, ผ้าไหม silk, silk cloth
mai-kwam wa หมายความว่า to mean
mak มาก very, a lot
mao เมา drunk, high
maw หมอ doctor
mee มี to have; there is, there exists
men เหม็น bad-smelling
meua-rai เมื่อไหร่ when
meuan เหมือน the same as, like
meuang เมือง city, town, country
meuay เมื่อย tired (*physically*)
meun หมื่น ten thousand
meut มืด dark (*no light*)
mia เมีย wife (*informal term*)
mia noi เมียน้อย mistress
moo หมู pig; pork
moo-ban หมู่บ้าน village
mot หมด all, all gone, used up
mot มด ant
mun มัน it; oil, oily, rich (*food*); potato

N

na **นา** rice field, farm field

nâ **หน้า** season

nâ **หน้า** face, front, in front of

nâ jà **น่าจะ** should

nâ **น่า** *prefix meaning* "worthy of"

nâ glua **น่ากลัว** frightening

nâ rak **น่ารัก** cute

nae, nae-jai **แน่, แน่ใจ** sure, certain, surely

nai **ใน** in, inside

nai **ไหน** where (*shortened form*), which (*following classifier*)

nak **หนัก** heavy, heavily

nak **นัก** *prefix meaning* "a person who"

nak gee-la **นักกีฬา** athlete

na-lee-ga **นาฬิกา** clock, watch; o'clock

nam **น้ำ** water, liquid

nan **นาน** a long time

nan **นั่น** that, those (*referring to things or people*)

nan **นั้น** that ("that hotel")

nang **นั่ง** to sit

nang **หนัง** skin, hide, leather; movie

nang -seu **หนังสือ** book, magazine

nang -seu phim **หนังสือพิมพ์** newspaper

nao **หนาว** cold (feeling/weather)

nap-theu **นับถือ** to respect, to believe in

na-thee **นาที** minute

na-thee **หน้าที่** duty

nawk **นอก** outside, foreign

nawk-jak **นอกจาก** besides, unless, except

nawn **นอน** to lie down, to sleep

nee **นี่** this, these

nee **นี้** this ("this shirt")

nee **หนี** to run away (from)

nee-sai **นิสัย** behavior, manners, character

nee-yom **นิยม** to like (something popular)

neua **เนื้อ** meat

neuaj **เหนือ** north (of), above

neuay **เหนื่อย** tired (*mentally*)

neung **หนึ่ง** one

noi **หน่อย** a little, somewhat (*adverb*)

noi **น้อย** a little (amount)

noom **หนุ่ม** young man; young (*to describe a man*)

noom **นุ่ม** soft (to the touch)

nuat **นวด** to massage

NG

ngai **ง่าย** easy, easily, simply

ngan **งาน** work, task, job; party, festival, fair

ngaoj **เหงา** lonely

ngeuhn **เงิน** money, silver

ngiap **เงียบ** quiet, quietly

ngong **งง** confused, perplexed

nguang nawn **ง่วงนอน** sleepy

O

o-gat **โอกาส** chance, opportunity

ong-saj **องศา** degree (*temperature*)

ot **อด** to go without, to starve

P

pa **ป่า** forest

pa **ป้า** aunt

paet **แปด** eight

pai **ไป** to go; too (*as in "too hot"*)

pai ป้าย sign (signboard)

pan-haj ปัญหา problem

pee ปี year

pen เป็น to be, can, able to

peuht เปิด to open, to turn on

pit ปิด to close, to turn off, to cover

plae แปล to translate, to mean (*when translated*)

plaek แปลก strange

plao เปล่า blank, void, empty

plawm ปลอม fake, counterfeit

plian เปลี่ยน to change

plook ปลุก to wake someone up

plook ปลูก to plant (tree, crops); to build (a house)

pok-ga-tee ปกติ normal, as usual, usually

praeng แปรง to brush; brush (*n*)

pra-jam ประจำ regular, regularly; always,
   permanent

pra-man ประมาณ about, approximately

pra-phay-nee ประเพณี custom, tradition

pra-thet ประเทศ country

prio เปรี้ยว sour

PH

pha, pha pai พา, พาไป to take (someone to a
   place)

pha ผ้า cloth

pha tat ผ่าตัด to operate (on the body)

phaeng แพง expensive

phak ผัก vegetable(s)

phak ภาค part, section, region

phak พัก to stay; period of time

phak-phawn พักผอน to rest, to relax

phak พรรค political party

phan **พัน** thousand

phan **ผ่าน** to pass through, to pass by

phao **เผ่า** tribe

phao **เผา** to burn (*do actively*)

pha-sa **ภาษา** language

phat **ผัด** to stir-fry

phat **พัด** to blow (wind, fan)

phat-tha-na **พัฒนา** to develop

phaw **พอ** enough

phaw **พอ** father

phawm **ผอม** thin, emaciated

pha-ya-yam **พยายาม** to try, to make an effort

phee **พี่** *title for older person*

phee **ผี** ghost

phee-set **พิเศษ** special, specially

phet **เผ็ด** hot, spicy

phet **เพศ** sex, gender

phet **เพชร** diamond

pheua **เผื่อ** in case, as a contingency

pheua **เพื่อ** in order to, so that, for the sake of

pheuan **เพื่อน** friend, acquaintance

pheuhm **เพิ่ม** to increase, to add on

phit **ผิด** wrong; different; guilty

phit, mee phit **พิษ, มีพิษ** poisonous

phlayng **เพลง** song

phom **ผม** I, me (*for men*); hair (on the head)

phoo-chai **ผู้ชาย** man

phoo-kao **ภูเขา** mountain

phoo-ying **ผู้หญิง** woman

phoot **พูด** to speak, to talk, to say

phop **พบ** to meet

phra **พระ** monk, lord, god, *title for sacred things*

phra a-thit **พระอาทิตย์** sun

phra jan **พระจันทร์** moon

phraw wa **เพราะว่า** because

phrawm **พร้อม** ready, completed; at the same time

R

ra-bop **ระบบ** system

ra-dap **ระดับ** level (*n*)

raek **แรก** first (in a series), beginning

raeng **แรง** strength, power, force, strongly

rai **ไร่** plantation; *unit of land measurement*

rai-gan **รายการ** program, list

rai-ngan **รายงาน** report (*n*); to report

rak **รัก** to love

ra-ka **ราคา** price

rak-sa **รักษา** to cure, to treat, to protect, to
  convalesce

ran **ร้าน** shop, store

rao **เรา** we, us

rap **รับ** to receive, to pick up, to catch

rap-phit-chawp **รับผิดชอบ** to be responsible (for)

rat **รัฐ** state (*as in* United States)

rat-tha-ban **รัฐบาล** government

raw **รอ** to wait (for)

ra-wang **ระวัง** to be careful

ra-wang **ระหว่าง** between, during

rawn **ร้อน** hot (*temperature*)

rawng **ร้อง** to cry out, to shout

rawng hai **ร้องไห้** to cry

rawng phlayng **ร้องเพลง** to sing

rawp **รอบ** to go around, cycle, lap, surrounding

reo **เร็ว** fast; early, soon

reu **หรือ** or

reuang เรื่อง about, subject, situation, story

reuay-reuay เรื่อยๆ continuously

reuhȷ เหรอ really?, oh?

reuhm เริ่ม to start, to originate

riak เรียก to call, is called

rian เรียน to study, to learn, to go to school

riap-roi เรียบร้อย in order, ready, neat, well-
mannered

roi ร้อย hundred

rom ลม shade, umbrella

rong-rian โรงเรียน school

roo รู hole

roo รู้ to know

roo-jak รู้จัก to know (a person/place)

roon รุ่น model; generation, age group, period

roop รูป picture; form, shape

roo-seuk รู้สึก to feel

rop-guan รบกวน to bother, to disturb

rot, rot chat รส, รสชาติ taste, flavor

rot รถ vehicle, car

rot รด to water (plants), to sprinkle water on

ruam รวม to put together, to combine

ruam ร่วม to do together, to share, mutual

ruay รวย rich, wealthy

S

sa-at สะอาด clean

sa-bai สบาย well, comfortable, easily

sa-daeng แสดง to show; show (n)

sa-duak สะดวก convenient

saenȷ แสน hundred thousand

sai ทราย sand

sai ใส่ to put in, to put on, to wear

sai ซ้าย left (side)

sai สาย late, late morning

sai สาย route, channel

sak, mai sak สัก, ไม้สัก teak wood

sak สัก to tattoo

sak ซัก to wash, to launder

saj-la ศาลา pavilion, hall

sam สาม three

sa-mai สมัย time period, age, era

sa-mat สามารถ to be able to (*formal*)

sam-rap สำหรับ for, designated for, as for

sa-nam สนาม field (sports, landing)

sang สั่ง to order

sang สร้าง to build

sa-nit สนิท tight, tightly; completely; intimate

sa-nook สนุก fun, enjoyable; to enjoy

sao, wan sao เสาร์, วันเสาร์ Saturday

sao สาว girl; young (*to describe a woman*)

sap-da สัปดาห์ week

sat สัตว์ animal

sa-thaj-nee สถานี station

sa-thanj-thee สถานที่ place

sat-sa-naj ศาสนา religion

sawm สอม fork

sawm ซ่อม to fix, to repair

sawm ซ้อม to practice

sawn ซ่อน to hide

sawn สอน to teach, to train

sawng ซอง envelope, packet

sawng สอง two

sawp สอบ to take a test

sayt-tha-git เศรษฐกิจ economy

see สี่ four

see **สี** color; paint (*n*)

sen **เส้น** line, strand, *classifier for things in strands*

set **เสร็จ** finished, ready, completed

seu **ซื้อ** to buy

seua **เสื่อ** mat

seua **เสื้อ** shirt

seua pha **เสื้อผ้า** clothes, clothing

seua **เสือ** tiger

seuk-sa **ศึกษา** to study (at a high level)

seu-sat **ซื่อสัตย์** honest

sia **เสีย** to lose, to waste, to use; broken, spoiled, polluted

sia-dai **เสียดาย** unhappy (from losing something)

sia-jai **เสียใจ** unhappy, sorry

siang **เสียง** sound, noise, sound of

sing **สิ่ง** a thing, things, something

sing **สิงห์** mythical lion (Singha)

sing-waet-lawm **สิ่งแวดล้อม** environment

sip **สิบ** ten

soi **ซอย** lane, side street; to cut into small pieces

soi kaw **สร้อยคอ** necklace

som-moot wa **สมมุติว่า** suppose that

song **ส่ง** to send

song-kram **สงคราม** war

song-sai wa **สงสัยว่า** to suspect that, to wonder if

song-san **สงสาร** to pity

son-jai **สนใจ** to be interested, to be interested in

soo **สู้** to fight, to struggle, to compete

sook **สุก** ripe; cooked until done

sook, wan sook **ศุกร์, วันศุกร์** Friday

sook-ka-phap **สุขภาพ** health

soon̯ **ศูนย์** center, headquarters; zero

soong̯ **สูง** tall, high

soop **สูบ** to smoke, to draw on; to pump

soo-phap **สุภาพ** polite

soot-thai **สุดท้าย** last (of a sequence), final,
  previous

sot **สด** fresh, uncooked

sot **โสด** single, unmarried

suan **ส่วน** part (of something)

suan mak **ส่วนมาก** most, mostly, usually

suan̯ **สวน** garden, park

suay **ซวย** bad luck

suay̯ **สวย** beautiful

sun **สั่น** to shake, to tremble

sun **สั้น** short (in length)

sun̯-ya **สัญญา** to promise, to contract; contract (*n*)

T

ta **ตา** eye

tae **แต่** but, only (*one kind, one thing*)

tae la **แต่ละ** each, every

taek **แตก** to break, to shatter, to burst, to split;
  broken

taek-tang **แตกต่าง** to differ

taeng **แตง** to decorate

taeng-ngan **แต่งงาน** to marry, to be married

tai **ตาย** to die

tai **ใต้** south (of), under, below

tak **ตาก** to expose to, to be exposed to

ta-lat **ตลาด** market

tam **ตาม** to follow, along

tam **ต่ำ** low

tang ต่าง different, to differ, separately

tang hak ต่างหาก separately, instead

tang pra-thet ต่างประเทศ foreign

tang-tang ต่างๆ various

tang ตั้ง to set up, to establish

tang-tae ตั้งแต่ since

tat ตัด to cut

taw ต่อ next, further, to extend, toward; per

ta-wan ตะวัน sun (*poetic, used in directions*)

tawn ตอน when, at (*for time*)

tawng ต้อง must, have to, should

tawng-gan ต้องการ would like, would like to, need

tee ตี to hit, to beat, to fight

tem เต็ม full, full of, whole

tia เตี้ย short (*in height*)

tit ติด to attach, to be attached to, to connect; to be addicted (to)

tok ตก to fall, to fall down, to drop

ton ต้น beginning, source; *classifier for plants*

ton-mai ต้นไม้ tree, plant

too ตู้ compartment, cabinet

trong ตรง straight, direct, directly

truat ตรวจ to inspect, to examine

tua ตัว body; *classifier for clothes, furniture and animals*

tuaj ตั๋ว ticket

TH

tha ทา to spread on

tha ถ้า if

tha reua ท่าเรือ pier

thae แท้ genuine, real

thaen **แทน** to substitute, to replace; instead (of)

thaeo **แถว** near; row

tham **ทำ** to do, to make, to cause

tham hai **ทำให้** to cause, to make (someone do something)

tham **ถ้ำ** cave

tham **ถาม** to ask

tham-ma-chat **ธรรมชาติ** nature, natural

tham-ma-da **ธรรมดา** regular, ordinary, usually, regularly

tham-mai **ทำไม** why

tham-ngan **ทำงาน** to work

than **ทัน** on time, in time

than **ทาน** to eat (*polite*)

than **ถาน** battery; charcoal

thang **ทาง** way, means, route, road, direction

thang-mot **ทั้งหมด** all, altogether

thang sawng **ทั้งสอง** both

thang **ถัง** barrel, bucket

tha-non **ถนน** road, street

thao, see thao **เทา, สีเทา** gray

thao **เท่า** equal, the same (*size, quantity*)

thao-gan **เท่ากัน** equal to each other

thao-nan **เท่านั้น** only, just, only that

thao-rai **เท่าไหร** how much

thao **เท้า** foot

thawng **ทอง** gold

thawng **ท้อง** abdomen

thawt **ถอด** to take off (shoes, clothing)

thawt **ทอด** to fry; fried

thee **ที** time, occasion

thee **ที่** place; at, that, which, who (*relative pn.*)

thee-din **ที่ดิน** land (piece of land)

thee-nai ที่ไหน where

thee-nee ที่นี่ here, this place

thee sawng ที่สอง second (*number two*)

theu ถือ to hold, to believe, to consider as

theung ถึง to arrive, to reach to, up to

thing ทิ้ง to throw away, to desert, to abandon

thio เที่ยว to visit, to travel, to go out

thon ทน to last (a long time), to endure

thook ถูก cheap; correct; to touch

thook ทุก each, every

thook yang ทุกอย่าง every kind, everything

thoong ถุง bag, sack

thoong na ทุ่งนา farm fields (*empty*)

thua ทั่ว throughout, all over

U

uan อ้วน fat; well-built

un อัน one, a thing, item; *general classifier for things*

un nee อันนี้ this one

W

wa ว่า that (*as in* "I said that"), to say, to think, to plan

waen แหวน ring

waen ta แว่นตา eyeglasses

wai ไหว้ *Thai greeting*

wai ไว้ to keep, to save; to put; to leave

wai ไหว able to do (*physically*)

wai-jai ไว้ใจ to trust

wai-nam ว่ายน้ำ to swim

wai-roon วัยรุ่น teenager

wan วัน day

wanj หวาน sweet

wang วาง to put down (object)

wang วาง free, not busy; vacant

wang wa หวังว่า to hope that

wat วาด to draw, to paint (a picture)

wat วัด to measure

wat วัด temple compound

wat-tha-na-tham วัฒนธรรม culture

way-la เวลา time

wing วิ่ง to run

wi-thee วิธี way, method, means

wong วง circle; group; *classifier for circular objects*

woon-wai วุ่นวาย to be busy with, confusing, in confusion

Y

ya ยา medicine

ya อย่า don't

ya หย่า to divorce

ya หญ้า grass

yae แย่ awful, terrible

yaek แยก to separate, to go apart

yai ใหญ่ big

yai ย้าย to move (*to live in another place*)

yak อยาก to want to

yak ยาก hard, difficult

yak ยักษ์ giant, ogre

yang ยัง still, yet

yang ยาง rubber

yang อย่าง kind, type; as

yang ย่าง barbecued

yang-rai, yang-ngai **อย่างไร, ยังไง** how (*first is formal pronunciation*)

yang-ngee **ยังงี้** like this, this kind

yao **ยาว** long (in length)

yat **ญาติ** relative

yawt **ยอด** peak

yee-haw **ยี่ห้อ** brand (brandname)

yen **เย็น** cold, cool (things)

yeuh **เยอะ** a lot

yeum **ยืม** to borrow

yim **ยิ้ม** to smile

yok **ยก** to lift, to raise; round (*in boxing*)

yoo **อยู่** to be at, to live at, to stay at

yoong **ยุง** mosquito

yoong **ยุ่ง** confusing, entangled, involved; to involve

yoot **หยุด** to stop

ENGLISH-THAI
DICTIONARY

A

a few สองสาม [sawng sam]

a little นิดหน่อย [nit noi]

a lot มาก, เยอะ [mak, yeuh]

abbreviation คำย่อ [kam yaw]

ability คำสมาส [kwam sa-mat]

able to ได้ [dai]

abortion (*to abort*) ทำแท้ง [tham thaeng]

about (*approximately*) ประมาณ [pra-man]

above (*on top*) บน, ข้างบน [bon, kang bon];
   (*over*) เหนือ [neua]

accent (*in speaking*) สำเนียง [sam-niang]

accident อุบัติเหตุ [oo-bat-tee-hayt]

accustomed to ... ชินกับ ... [chin gap ...]

act (*v*) แสดง [sa-daeng]

activity, activities กิจกรรม [git-ja-gam]

add บวก [buak]

add to (*put in*) เติม [teuhm]

add up (*put together*) รวม [ruam]

addicted (to) ติด [tit]

addictive drug ยาเสพติด [ya sayp-tit]

adjust ปรับ [prap]

administrate บริหาร [baw-ree-han]

administration การบริหาร [gan-baw-ree-han]

advertise, advertisement โฆษณา [kot-sa-na]

advise แนะนำ [nae-nam]

afraid กลัว [glua]

again อีก [eeg]; (*newly*) ใหม่ [mai]

agency องค์การ [ong-gan]

agree (*after negotiations*) ตกลง [tok-long];
   (*~ with an opinion*) เห็นด้วย [hen duay]

agriculture เกษตรศาสตร์ [ga-sayt-sat]

air อากาศ [a-gat]; (*for tires*) ลม [lom]

air-conditioned แอร์, ปรับอากาศ [ae, prap a-gat]

air conditioner เครื่องแอร์ [kreuang ae]

air pollution อากาศเสีย [a-gat siaj]

airplane เครื่องบิน [kreuang bin]

airplane crash เครื่องบินตก [kreuang bin tok]

alike (*similar*) คล้ายๆกัน [klai-klai gan]; (*the same*) เหมือนกัน [meuanj-gan]

alive มีชีวิต, เป็นๆ [mee chee-wit, pen-pen]

all ทั้งหมด [thang-mot]

all gone (*used up*) หมด [mot]

allow ให้, อนุญาต [hai, a-noo-yat]

almost เกือบ [geuap]

alone คนเดียว [kon dio]

alphabet ตัวอักษร [tua ak-sawnj]

alright (*adequate*) พอใช้ได้ [phaw chai dai]; (*would be okay*) ก็ได้ [gaw dai]

also (*in addition*) ด้วย [duay]; (*the same*) เหมือนกัน [meuanj-gan]; (*together*) ด้วยกัน [duay-gan]

altitude ความสูง [kwam-soongj]

altogether ทั้งหมด [thang-mot]

amount จำนวน [jam-nuan]

amphetamine ยาบ้า [ya ba]

analyze วิเคราะห์ [wee-kraw]

ancestors บรรพบุรุษ [ban-pha-boo-root]

ancient โบราณ, เก่าแก่ [bo-ran, gao-gae]

and (*formal*) และ [lae]

Angkor Wat นครวัด [Na-kawn Wat]

angry โกรธ [grot]; (*suddenly*) โมโห [mo-hoj]

announce, announcement ประกาศ [pra-gat]

another (*more*) อีก [eeg]; (*some other*) อื่น [(*classifier*) eun]

answer (*respond*) ตอบ [tawp]; (*~ the phone*) รับ [rap]

antenna เสาอากาศ [sao a-gat]

antique(s) ของเก่า [kawng gao]

apologize ขอโทษ [kaw thot]

apply (for job) สมัคร [sa-mak]

appropriate เหมาะสม [maw som]

approximately ประมาณ [pra-man]

archaeology โบราณคดี [bo-ran-na-ka-dee]

area บริเวณ [baw-ree-wayn]; (*zone*) เขต [kayt]

argue ทะเลาะ [tha-law]

arrange จัด [jat]

arrest จับ [jap]

art, the arts ศิลปะ [sin-la-pa]

as usual ตามปกติ, ตามธรรมดา [tam pok-ga-tee, tam tham-ma-da]

ask ถาม [tham]

ask for something ขอ [kaw]

ask for permission ขออนุญาต [kaw a-noo-yat]

atmosphere (*air*) อากาศ [a-gat]; (*ambiance*) บรรยากาศ [ban-ya-gat]

attach, attached ติด [tit]

attack (*~ a person*) ทำร้าย [tham-rai]; (*invade*) บุก, บุกรุก [book, book-rook]

B

bachelor ชายโสด [chai sot]

bachelor's degree ปริญญาตรี [prin-ya tree]

bad (*awful*) แย่ [yae]; (*not good*) ไม่ดี [mai dee]; (*~ person*) ชั่ว, ร้าย [chua, rai]

bad-acting นิสัยไม่ดี [nee-sai mai dee]

bad luck ซวย, โชคร้าย [suay, chok rai]

bad mood อารมณ์ไม่ดี [a-rom mai dee]

bad-smelling เหม็น [měn]

bag (*sack*) ถุง [thǒong]; (*suitcase, purse*) กระเป๋า [gra-pǎo]

bald หัวล้าน [hǔa lán]

ball บอล [bawn]

bamboo (*wood*) ไม้ไผ่ [mái phài]

banana tree ต้นกล้วย [tôn glúay]

band (*music*) วงดนตรี [wong don-tree]

Bangkok กรุงเทพฯ [Groong-thâyp]

bargain (*v*) ต่อ, ต่อรอง [tàw, tàw rawng]

bark (*dog's*) เห่า [hào]

basket ตะกร้า [ta-grâ]

bathe อาบน้ำ [àb-nam]

bathroom ห้องน้ำ [hâwng-nam]

battery (*for flashlight*) ถ่านไฟฉาย [thàn fai-chǎi];
  (*for vehicle*) แบตเตอรี่ [bàet-ta-rèe]

bay (*gulf*) อ่าว [ào]

be เป็น, คือ [pen, keu]

be at อยู่ [yòo]

be lost หลงทาง [lǒng thang]

beach หาดทราย, ชายหาด [hàt sai, chai hàt]

beat (*hit, strike*) ตี [tee]; (*rythmn*) จังหวะ [jang-wà];
  (*win*) ชนะ [cha-ná]

beautiful สวย [sǔay]; (*for music*) เพราะ [phráw];
  (*pretty*) งาม [ngam]

beg alms ขอทาน [kǎw than]

begin เริ่ม [rêuhm]

behavior นิสัย [nee-sǎi]

believe เชื่อ [chêua]

believe in นับถือ [náp-thěu]

bell ระฆัง [ra-kang]

below (*~ an area*) ล่าง, ข้างล่าง [lâng, kâng lâng];
  (*~ an object*) ใต้ [tâi]

besides นอกจาก [nawk-jak]

best ดีที่สุด [dee thee-soot]

better ดีกว่า [dee gwa]; (*improved*) ดีขึ้น [dee keun]

big ใหญ่ [yai]

birth control (*v*) (*to control conception*) คุมกำเนิด [koom gam-neuht]; (*n*) การคุมกำเนิด [gan koom gam-neuht]

birthday วันเกิด [wan geuht]

bite กัด [gat]

bitter ขม [kom]

black สีดำ [see dam]

black market ตลาดมืด [ta-lat meut]

bland จืด [jeut]

bless อวยพร [uay-phawn]

blessing (*n*) พร [phawn]

blind ตาบอด [ta bawt]

blow (~ *from the mouth*) เป่า [pao]; (*wind, fan*) พัด [phat]

blue (*dark* ~) สีน้ำเงิน [see nam-ngeuhn]; (*light* ~) สีฟ้า [see fa]

board (*wood*) กระดาน [gra-dan]

body ตัว [tua]; (*corpse*) ศพ [sop]

boil (*boiled*) ต้ม [tom]; (*is boiling*) เดือด [deuat]

bomb (*v*) ทิ้งระเบิด [thing ra-beuht]; (*n*) ระเบิด [ra-beuht]

book หนังสือ [nang-seu]

border ชายแดน [chai-daen]

bored เบื่อ [beua]

boring น่าเบื่อ [na beua]

born เกิด [geuht]

borrow ยืม [yeum]

both ทั้งสอง [thang sawng]

bother (*n*) ลำบาก [lam-bak]; (*v*) รบกวน [rop-guan]

bothered (*feeling*) รำคาญ [ram-kan]

box (*n*) กล่อง [glawng]; (*v*) ชกมวย chok muay

boxing ring เวที [way-thee]

boyfriend แฟน [faen]

brake (*n*) เบรค [brayk]

branch (*~ of bank, etc*) สาขา [saj-kaj]

brand (brand name) ยี่ห้อ [yee-haw]

break (*rest from work*) พัก [phak]; (*~ in two*) หัก [hak]; (*not working, broken*) เสีย [siaj]; (*shatter, burst*) แตก [taek]

break up (*relationship*) เลิกกัน [leuhk gan]

breathe หายใจ [haij-jai]

bride เจ้าสาว [jao saoj]

bridegroom เจ้าบ่าว [jao bao]

bridge สะพาน [sa-phan]

bright (*light*) สว่าง [sa-wang]

bring (*~ a person*) พามา [pha ma]; (*~ an object*) เอามา [ao ma]

broad (*wide, spacious*) กว้าง [gwang]

broken (*~ in two*) หัก [hak]; (*not working*) เสีย [siaj]; (*shattered, burst*) แตก [taek]

broken-hearted อกหัก [ok hak]

brothel ซ่อง [sawng]

brown สีน้ำตาล [seej nam-tan]

brush (*n/v*) แปรง [praeng]

brush one's teeth แปรงฟัน [praeng fun]

budget (*n*) งบประมาณ [ngop pra-man]

build สร้าง [sang]

building (*concrete ~*) ตึก [teuk]

bullet ลูกปืน [look peun]

bump into ชน [chon]

burn (*do actively*) เผา [phǎo]; (*is burning*) ไหม้ [mâi]

bury ฝัง [fǎng]

buy ซื้อ [séu]

C

cage กรง [grong]

calculate คิด [kít]

calendar ปฏิทิน [pà-tee-thin]

call เรียก [rîak]; (*~ on a phone*) โทรไป [tho pai]

camera กล้องถ่ายรูป [glâwng thài roop]

can (*able to*) ได้, เป็น [dâi, pen]; (*n*) (*tin ~*) กระป๋อง [grà-pǎwng]

can't find หาไม่เจอ [hǎa mâi jeuh]

can't sleep นอนไม่หลับ [nawn mâi làp]

canal คลอง [klawng]

candle เทียน [thian]

capital city เมืองหลวง [meuang lǔang]

carry (*hold*) ถือ [thěu]; (*~ a suitcase/bucket*) หิ้ว [hîu]

cart เกวียน [gwian]

cartoon การ์ตูน [ga-toon]

carve แกะสลัก [gàe sà-làk]

casket หีบศพ [hèep sòp]

catch จับ [jàp]

cause (*n*) สาเหตุ [sǎo-hàyt]

cause to ... ทำให้ ... [tham hâi ...]

cave ถ้ำ [thâm]

CD แผ่นดิส [phàen dìt]

celebrate ฉลอง [cha-lawng]

cement ปูน [poon]

cemetery (*Chinese*) สุสาน [sǒo-sǎng]; (*Thai*) ป่าช้า [pà-cháa]

center (*headquarters*) ศูนย์ [soon]; (*middle*) กลาง [glang]

centimeter เซนติเมตร, เซน [sen-ti-met, sen]

century ศตวรรษ [sat-ta-wat]

ceremony พิธี [phee-thee]

chain โซ่ [so]

chance โอกาส [o-gat]

change (*v*) เปลี่ยน [plian]

change one's mind เปลี่ยนใจ [plian jai]

channel ช่อง [chawng]

chapter บท [bot]

characteristic(s) ลักษณะ [lak-sa-na]

charcoal ถ่าน [than]

chase after ไล่ตาม [lai tam]

cheap ถูก [thook]

cheat (*deceive*) หลอก, หลอกหลวง [lawk, lawk luang]; (*~ for money*) โกง [gong]

check (*v*) ตรวจ [truat]

chemical สารเคมี [san-kay-mee]

chew เคี้ยว [kio]

chew betel กินหมาก [gin mak]

child, children (*in general*) เด็ก [dek]; (*of your own*) ลูก [look]

choose เลือก [leuak]

cigarette บุหรี่ [boo-ree]

cigarette lighter ไฟแช็ค [fai chaek]

city เมือง [meuang]

clap hands ตบมือ [top meu]

class (*level*) ชั้น [chan]

classroom ห้องเรียน [hawng rian]

clean (*adj*) สะอาด [sa-at]; (*v*) ทำความสะอาด [tham kwam sa-at]

clear, clearly ชัด [chat]

clever ฉลาด [cha-lat]

climate อากาศ [a-gat]

climb ปีน [peen]

clock นาฬิกา [na-lee-ga]

close (v) ปิด [pit]

closed ปิดแล้ว [pit laeo]

cloth ผ้า [pha]

clothes เสื้อผ้า [seua pha]

coast (*n*) ฝั่งทะเล [fang tha-lay]

cold (*feeling, weather*) หนาว [nao]; (*things*)
   เย็น [yen]

collect (*accumulate*) สะสม [sa-som]; (*pick up
   things*) เก็บ [gep]

college วิทยาลัย [wit-tha-ya-lai]

colony เมืองขึ้น, อาณานิคม [meuang keun,
   a-na-nee-kom]

color สี [see]

comb หวี [wee]

comb one's hair หวีผม [wee phom]

come มา [ma]

come back กลับมา [glap ma]

come from มาจาก [ma jak]

come in เข้ามา [kao ma]

come out ออก [awk]

comfortable สบาย [sa-bai]

comet ดาวหาง [dao hang]

commerce การค้า [gan ka]

committee คณะกรรมการ [ka-na gam-ma-gan]

compare เปรียบเทียบ [priap thiap]

compass เข็มทิศ [kem thit]

compete แข่ง, แข่งขัน [kaeng, kaeng-kun]

competition การแข่งขัน [gan-kaeng-kun]

complain บ่น [bon]

complete (*adj*) (*includes everything*) ครบ [krop]

completed (*finished*) เสร็จแล้ว [set laeo]

complicated (*detailed*) ละเอียด [la-iat]; (*hard to understand*) ซับซ้อน [sup-sawn]

computer คอมพิวเตอร์ [kawm-phiu-teuh]

concentration สมาธิ [sa-ma-thee]

concerned (*worried*) เป็นห่วง [pen huang]

concert คอนเสิร์ต [kawn-seuht]

condition (*state*) สภาพ [sa-phap]

condom ถุงยาง [thoong yang]

confident มั่นใจ [mun-jai]

confirm ยืนยัน [yeun-yan]

confused งง, สับสน [ngong, sup-song]

confusing สับสน [sup-song]

consciousness สติ [sa-tee]

conserve รักษา, อนุรักษ์ [rak-sa, a-noo-rak]

consideration for others เกรงใจ [grayng-jai]

consonant (*letter*) พยัญชนะ [pha-yan-cha-na]

constitution (*of a gov't*) รัฐธรรมนูญ [rat-tha-tham-ma-noon]

construct สร้าง [sang]

construction ก่อสร้าง [gaw sang]

consult ปรึกษา [preuk-sa]

contact (*v*) ติดต่อ [tit-taw]

contest (*v*) ประกวด [pra-guat]

continent ทวีป [tha-weep]

continuously เรื่อยๆ [reuay-reuay]

contract (*n/v*) สัญญา [sun-ya]

control (*supervise*) ควบคุม, คุม [kuap-koom, koom]

convenient สะดวก [sa-duak]

cook (*v*) ทำอาหาร, ทำกับข้าว [tham a-han, tham gap kao]

cook rice หุงข้าว [hoong kao]

cool เย็น [yen]

cooperate ร่วมมือ [ruam meu]

copy (*counterfeit*) ปลอม [plawm]; (*photo*) อัด [at]

copyright (*n*) ลิขสิทธิ์ [lik-ka-sit]

coral ปะการัง [pa-ga-rang]

corner มุม [moom]

corpse ศพ [sop]

correct, correctly ถูก, ถูกต้อง [thook, thook-tawng]

correct (*adj*) (*for time*) ตรง [trong]; (*v*) แก้, แก้ไข [gae, gae kai]

corrupt คอรัปชั่น [kaw-rup-chan]

count (*v*) นับ [nap]

country ประเทศ [pra-thet]

countryside บ้านนอก, ชนบท [ban nawk, chon-na-bot]

coup d'etat การปฏิวัติ [gan-pa-tee-wat]

court (*flirt*) จีบ [jeep]; (*go to ~ of law*) ขึ้นศาล [keun san]

cover (*n*) ฝา [fa]; (*v*) ปิด, คลุม [pit, kloom]

cramped แคบ [kaep]

crash (*v*) ชน [chon]

crazy บ้า [ba]

crazy and silly บ้าๆ บอๆ [ba-ba-baw-baw]

credit (*money*) เงินผ่อน [ngeuhn phawn]

cremate เผาศพ [phao sop]

criminal นักเลง [nak layng]

criticize (*critique*) วิจารณ์ [wee-jan]; (*say bad things*) ติ [tee]

cross (*go across*) ข้าม [kam]

crowded (*many people*) คนมาก, แออัด [kon

mak, ae-at]; (*tightly-packed*) แน่น [naen]

cry ร้องไห้ [rawng hai]

cry out ร้อง [rawng]

culture วัฒนธรรม [wat-tha-na-tham]

cure รักษา [rak-saj]

curve, curved โค้ง [kong]

custom (*tradition*) ประเพณี [pra-phay-nee]

customer ลูกค้า [look ka]

cut ตัด [tat]; (*finger, etc*) บาด [bat]

cut down trees ตัดไม้ [tat mai]

cut one's hair ตัดผม [tat phomj]

cute น่ารัก [na rak]

D

dam (*n*) เขื่อน [keuan]

dance เต้น [ten]

dangerous อันตราย [an-ta-rai]

dare (*v*) กล้า [glaj]

dark (*color*) แก่ [gae]; (*skin*) ดำ [dam]; (*no light*) มืด [meut]

data ข้อมูล [kaw-moon]

dead ตายแล้ว, เสียชีวิต [tai laeo, siaj chee-wit]

deaf หูหนวก [hooj nuak]

debt หนี้สิน [nee-sinj]

decide ตัดสินใจ [tat-sinj-jai]

decimal point จุด [joot]

decorate แต่ง, ตกแต่ง [taeng, tok taeng]

decrease ลง [long]

deep ลึก [leuk]; (*profound*) ลึกซึ้ง [leuk-seung]

defecate ถ่าย [thai]

defend ป้องกัน [pawng-gan]

definitely แน่นอน [nae-nawn]

degree (*temperature*) องศา [ong-saj]

delicious อร่อย [a-roi]

democratic ประชาธิปไตย [pra-cha-thip-pa-tai]

demolish ทุบทิ้ง [thoop thing]

deny ปฏิเสธ [pa-tee-sayt]

department (*gov't*) หน่วยงาน, กรม, กอง [nuay-ngan, grom, gawng]

depends on ... ขึ้นกับ ..., แล้วแต่ ... [keun gap..., laeo tae...]

deposit (*when renting*) มัดจำ [mat-jam]

depressed (*unhappy*) กลุ้มใจ [gloom-jai]

desert ทะเลทราย [tha-lay sai]

design (*n*) แบบ [baep]; (*on cloth, etc*) ลาย [lai]; (*v*) ออกแบบ [awk baep]

destroy ทำลาย [tham-lai]

detail(s) ลายละเอียด [rai-la-iat]

detailed ละเอียด [la-iat]

develop (*upgrade*) พัฒนา [phat-tha-na]

developed พัฒนาแล้ว [phat-tha-na laeo]; (*prosperous*) เจริญ [ja-reuhn]

dictator เผด็จการ [pha-det-gan]

dictionary พจนานุกรม [pot-ja-na-noo-grom]

die (*v*) ตาย, เสียชีวิต [tai, sia chee-wit]

different ไม่เหมือน [mai meuan]

different from each other ไม่เหมือนกัน, ต่างกัน [mai meuan gan, tang gan]

difficult (*a bother*) ลำบาก [lam-bak]; (*hard*) ยาก [yak]

dig (*v*) ขุด [koot]

dike (*n*) เขื่อน [keuan]

direct, directly ตรง [trong]

direction (*compass*) ทิศ [thit]; (*way*) ทาง [thang]

dirt ดิน [din]

dirty ไม่สะอาด, สกปรก [mai sa-at, sok-ga-prok]

disagree ไม่เห็นด้วย [maí henj duay]

disappear หาย [haij]

disappointed ผิดหวัง [phìt wangj]

disk แผ่นดิส [phàen dìt]

distribute (*give out*) แจก [jaek]; (*sell*) จำหน่าย [jam-naì]

dive ดำน้ำ [dam nam]

divide up แบ่งกัน [baeng gàn]

divorce หย่า [ya]

divorced from each other แยกกัน, หย่ากัน [yaek gàn, ya gàn]

do ทำ [tham]

doctorate ปริญญาเอก [prin-ya ayk]

document เอกสาร [ayk-ga-sanj]

doll ตุ๊กตา [took-ga-ta]

donate บริจาค [baw-ree-jak]

dormitory หอพัก [hawj phak]

doubt สงสัย [songj-saij]

down ลง [long]

dozen โหล [loj]

draft into the army เกณฑ์ทหาร [gayn tha-hanj]

dragon มังกร [mung-gawn]

drama (*play, TV*) ละคร [la-kawn]

draw วาด [wat]

draw a picture วาดรูป [wat roop]

dream ฝัน [funj]

dress (*get dressed*) ใส่เสื้อผ้า [saì seua-phà]

drink กิน, ดื่ม [gin, deum]

drink liquor กินเหล้า [gin laò]

drive ขับ [kap]

drown จมน้ำ [jom-nam]

drum กลอง [glawng]

drunk เมา [mao]

dry แห้ง [haeng]; (*for places*) แล้ง, แห้งแล้ง [laeng, haeng-laeng]

dust ฝุ่น [foon]

duty หน้าที่ [na-thee]

dye (*v*) ย้อม [yawm]

E

each ... แต่ละ ... [tae la ...]

each other, do to กัน [(*v*) gan]

earth (*planet*) โลก [lok]

earthquake แผ่นดินไหว [phaen din wai]

east ตะวันออก [ta-wan awk]

easy (*no problem*) สบาย [sa-bai]

easy, easily ง่าย [ngai]

easy-going ใจเย็น, ใจง่าย [jai-yen, jai-ngai]

eat กิน, ทาน, รับประทาน [gin, than, rap-pra-than]

economy เศรษฐกิจ [sayt-tha-git]

education การศึกษา [gan seuk-sa]

elect เลือก [leuak]

election การเลือกตั้ง [gan leuak-tang]

electricity ไฟ, ไฟฟ้า [fai, fai fa]

elementary school ประถมศึกษา [pra-thom seuk-sa]

embarrassed อาย [ai]

embrace กอด [gawt]

emotion อารมณ์ [a-rom]

empty เปล่า [plao]

end (*n*) สิ้น, ปลาย, ท้าย [sin, plai, thai]

endure อดทน [ot-thon]

enemy ศัตรู [sat-troo]

energy (*force, power*) กำลัง, พลัง [gam-lang, pha-lang]; (*strength*) แรง [raeng]

engage (*to marry*) หมั้น [mun]

engine เครื่องยนต์ [kreuang yon]

enough พอ [phaw]

enter เข้า [kao]

entertain (*guests*) รับรอง [rap-rawng]

entrust (*something to someone*) ฝาก [fak]

envelope ซองจดหมาย [sawng jot-mai]

envious อิจฉา [eet-cha]

environment สิ่งแวดล้อม [sing-waet-lawm]

envy อิจฉา [eet-cha]

equal (*to each other*) เท่ากัน [thao-gan]

equipment อุปกรณ์ [oop-pa-gawn]

erase ลบ [lop]

escape หนี [nee]

especially โดยเฉพาะ [doy cha-phaw]

ethnic group เชื้อชาติ [cheua chat]

even if ถึง, แม้ว่า [theung, mae wa]

event (*incident*) เหตุการณ์ [hayt-gan]

ever (*have ever*) เคย [keuy]

every ทุก, ทุกๆ [thook, thook-thook]

everybody ทุกคน [thook kon]

everything ทุกอย่าง [thook yang]

evidence หลักฐาน [lak-thang]

examination (*take an ~*) สอบ [sawp]

examine ตรวจ [truat]

example ตัวอย่าง [tua yang]

except นอกจาก [nawk-jak]

excited ตื่นเต้น [teun-ten]

excrement ขี้ [kee]

exercise (*v*) ออกกำลังกาย [awk gam-lang gai]

exhaust (*from a vehicle*) ควันรถ [kwan rot]

exhausted เพลีย [phlia]

expand ขยาย [ka-yai]

expect that ... คาดว่า ..., กะว่า ... [kat wa...,
    ga wa...]

expenses ค่าใช้จ่าย [ka chai-jai]

expensive แพง [phaeng]

experience (*n*) ประสบการณ์ [pra-sop-gan]; (*v*)
    ประสบ [pra-sop]

expert (*person*) ผู้เชี่ยวชาญ [phoo chio-chan]

expertly เก่ง [geng]

expired หมดอายุ [mot a-yoo]

explain อธิบาย [a-thee-bai]

explode ระเบิด [ra-beuht]

expose to ตาก [tak]

extend ต่อ [taw]

extinct (*become ~*) สูญพันธ์ [soon phan]

extinguish (*fire, light*) ดับ [dap]

extravagant ฟุ่มเฟือย [foom-feuay]

eyeglasses แว่นตา [waen ta]

F

fade (*colors*) สีตก [see tok]

fail an exam สอบตก [sawp tok]

fair (*equitable, just*) ยุติธรรม [yoot-tee-tham];
    (*festival*) งาน [ngan]

faithful (*in love*) ใจเดียว [jai-dio]

fake (*adj/v*) ปลอม [plawm]

fall (*drop down*) ตก [tok]

fall down, fall over ล้ม [lom]

famous ดัง, มีชื่อ [dang, mee cheu]

fan (*n*) พัดลม [phat-lom]

farm (*n*) (*garden*) สวน [suan], (*plantation*) ไร่
    [rai], (*rice field*) นา [na]; (*v*) (*~ rice*) ทำนา
    [tham na]

fashion แฟชั่น [fae-chun]

fast (*quick*) เร็ว, เร็วๆ [reo, reo-reo]; (*urgent, express*) ด่วน [duan]

fat (*adj*) อ้วน [uan]; (*n*) ไขมัน [kaij-mun]

feel รู้สึก [roo-seuk]

feeling (n) ความรู้สึก [kwam roo-seuk]

fence รั้ว [rua]

fertilizer ปุ๋ย [puij]

festival งาน, เทศกาล [ngan, thayt-sa-gan]

field (*farm*) นา, ทุ่งนา [na, thoong na]; (*sports, landing*) สนาม [sa-namj]

fight (*v*) (*have problem with a person*) มีเรื่อง [mee reuang]; (*in war*) รบ, สู้รบ [rop, soo-rop], (*hit, punch*) ตอย, ตี, ชก [toi, tee, chok], (*struggle*) สู้ [soo]

fight with each other ต่อยกัน, ตีกัน [toi gan, tee gan]

fill (a tooth) อุด [oot]

final สุดท้าย [soot-thai]

finally ในที่สุด [nai thee-soot]

find พบ, เจอ [phop, jeuh]

fine (*n*) (*for an infraction*) ปรับ [prap]; (*adj*) (*well*) สบายดี [sa-bai dee]

finish, make finished ทำให้เสร็จ [tham hai set]

finished (*a task*) เสร็จแล้ว [set laeo]; (*ended – a movie, etc*) จบ, จบแล้ว [jop, jop laeo]; (*used up*) หมด [mot]

fire (*n*) ไฟ [fai]; (*v*) (*~ from job*) ไล่ออก [lai awk]

first (*at first*) ตอนแรก [tawn raek]; (*before something else*) ก่อน [gawn]; (*in a progression*) แรก [(*classifier*) raek]

first class ชั้นหนึ่ง [chan neung]

fix (*repair*) ซ่อม [sawm]

flag (*of a country*) ธง, ธงชาติ [thong, thong chat]

flashlight ไฟฉาย [fai chaij]

flat (*for land*) ราบ [rap]; (*for objects*) แบน [baen]

flat tire ยางแบน [yang baen]

flavor รส, รสชาติ [rot, rot chat]

flirt จีบ [jeep]

float ลอย [loi]

floating market ตลาดน้ำ [ta-lat nam]

flood น้ำท่วม [nam thuam]

flour แป้ง [paeng]

flower ดอกไม้ [dawk-mai]

fly (*v*) บิน [bin]

follow ตาม [tam]

food อาหาร [a-hanj]

for (~ *the sake of*) เพื่อ [pheua]; (*to give to*) ให้, สำหรับ [hai, samj-rap]; (*to use* ~) ใช้ [chai]

force (*v*) บังคับ [bang-kap]

foreign ต่างประเทศ [tang pra-thet]

forest ป่า [pa]

forget ลืม [leum]

forgive ให้อภัย [hai a-phai]

form (*n*) (*paper to fill out*) ฟอร์ม [fawm]

formal ทางการ [thang-gan]

fragile แตกง่าย [taek ngai]

frame (*for a picture*) กรอบ [grawp]

free อิสระ [eet-sa-ra]; (*included with purchase*) แถม [thaemj]; (*no charge*) ฟรี [free]; (*not busy*) ว่าง [wang]

free time เวลาว่าง [way-la wang]

freedom อิสรภาพ [eet-sa-ra-phap]; (*liberty*)
เสรีภาพ [sayɼ-ree-phap]

fresh สด [sot]

fresh water น้ำจืด [nam jeut]

friend เพื่อน [pheuan]

friendly (*casual*) เป็นกันเอง [pen gan ayng];
(*kind*) ใจดี [jai-dee]

friends, to be คบกัน [kop gan]

friendship มิตรภาพ [mit-tra-phap]

frightened (*adj*) (*afraid*) กลัว [glua]; (*v*)
(*startled*) ตกใจ [tok-jai]

frightening น่ากลัว [na glua]

full (~ *container*) เต็ม [tem]; (*from eating*) อิ่ม
[im]

fun (*enjoyable*) สนุก [sa-nook]

funds ทุน [thoon]

funeral งานศพ [ngan sop]

funny ตลก [ta-lok]

fussy จู้จี้ [joo-jee]

future อนาคต [a-na-kot]

G

garbage ขยะ [ka-ya]

garden สวน [suanɼ]

gasoline น้ำมัน [nam-mun]

gender เพศ [phet]

generation รุ่น [roon]

generous มีน้ำใจ [mee nam-jai]

gentle อ่อน [awn]

gently ค่อยๆ [koi-koi]

genuine แท้ [thae]

get (*acquire*) ได้ [dai]; (*receive*) ได้, ได้รับ [dai,
dai rap]; (*take away*) เอา [ao]

get dressed ใส่เสื้อผ้า [sai seua-pha]

get in/on (a vehicle) ขึ้น [keun]

get lost หลงทาง [long thang]

get married แต่งงาน [taeng-ngan]

get out/off (of a vehicle) ลง [long]

get ready เตรียมตัว [triam tua]

get up ลุก, ลุกขึ้น [look, look keun]

get up from sleeping ตื่นนอน [teun nawn]

ghost ผี [phee]

gift ของขวัญ [kawng-kwan]

ginseng โสม [som]

girlfriend แฟน [faen]

give ให้, เอาให้ [hai, ao hai]

give an example ยกตัวอย่าง [yok tua yang]

give back คืน [keun]

glass (*drinking*) แก้ว [gaeo]; (*window*) กระจก [gra-jok]

glasses แวนตา [waen ta]

glue กาว [gao]

go ไป [pai]

go across ข้าม [kam]

go around รอบ [rawp]

go back กลับ [glap]

go down (*descend*) ลง [long]; (*reduce*) ลด [lot]

go home กลับบ้าน [glap ban]

go in เข้า [kao]

go out ออก [awk]

go out for fun ไปเที่ยว [pai thio]

go shopping ไปซื้อของ [pai seu kawng]

go to a movie ไปดูหนัง [pai doo nang]

go to school เรียนหนังสือ [rian nang-seu]

go to see (a person) ไปหา, เยี่ยม [pai ha, yiam]

go to see a doctor ไปหาหมอ [pai ha maw]

go to see a friend ไปหาเพื่อน [pai haj pheuan]

go to sleep นอน [nawn]

go to toilet เข้าห้องน้ำ [kao hawng-nam]

go up ขึ้น [keun]

goal (*objective*) จุดมุ่งหมาย [joot-moong-maij]

God พระเจ้า [Phra-jao]

godfather (*Mafia*) เจ้าพ่อ [jao phaw]

gold ทอง [thawng]

gold color สีทอง [seej thawng]

gone (*disappeared*) หาย [haij]; (*left already*) ไปแล้ว [pai laeo]; (*used up*) หมด [mot]

good ดี [dee]

good luck โชคดี [chok dee]

good mood อารมณ์ดี [a-rom dee]

good-smelling หอม [hawmj]

gossip (*mostly of bad things*) นินทา [nin-tha]

government (*local*) เทศบาล [thayt-sa-ban]; (*national*) รัฐบาล [rat-tha-ban]

grade (*level, class*) ชั้น [chan]

gradually ค่อยๆ [koi-koi]

graduate (*v*) เรียนจบ [rian jop]

grammar ไวยกรณ์ [wai-ya-gawn]

grass หญ้า [ya]

gray สีเทา [seej thao]

greedy โลภ, ละโมบ [lop, la-mop]; (*stingy*) งก [ngok]

green สีเขียว [seej kioj]

group (*music*) วงดนตรี [wong don-tree]; (*of people*) กลุ่ม [gloom]

grow (*about people*) โตขึ้น [to keun]; (*about plants*) ขึ้น [keun]

grown up โต [to]

guarantee (*n*) ประกัน [pra-gan]; (*v*) รับประกัน [rap-pra-gan]

guard (*v*) เฝ้า [fao]

guess เดา, ทาย [dao, thai]

guest แขก [kaek]

guilty (*for infraction*) ผิด [phit]

guitar กีต้าร์ [gee-ta]

gulf อ่าว [ao]

gum (*chewing*) หมากฝรั่ง [mak fa-rang]

gun ปืน [peun]

H

hair (*on the body*) ขน [kon]; (*on the head*) ผม [phom]

hairstyle ทรงผม [song phom]

half ครึ่ง [kreung (*classifier*)]; (*one-half*) ครึ่งหนึ่ง [kreung neung]

hammer ค้อน [kawn]

handbook คู่มือ [koo meu]

handicapped person คนพิการ [kon phee-gan]

handicrafts หัตถกรรม [hat-tha-gam]

handsome หล่อ [law]

handwriting ลายมือ [lai meu]

hang แขวน [kwaen]; (*~ by the neck*) แขวนคอ [kwaen kaw]

hangover เมาค้าง [mao kang]

happen เกิด, เกิดขึ้น [geuht, geuht keun]

happy (*general feeling*) มีความสุข [mee kwam-sook]; (*glad*) ดีใจ [dee-jai]

hard (*difficult*) ยาก [yak]; (*heavily*) หนัก [nak]; (*opp. of soft*) แข็ง [kaeng]

hard-working ขยัน [ka-yan]

harvest rice เกี่ยวข้าว [gio kao]

hate เกลียด [gliat]

have มี [mee]

have ever (done something) เคย [keuy]

have to ต้อง [tawng (*verb*)]

health สุขภาพ [sook-ka-phap]

healthy สุขภาพดี [sook-ka-phap dee]

hear ได้ดี [dai yin]

hear news ได้ยินข่าว [dai yin kao]

heart หัวใจ [huaj-jai]

heart and mind (*figurative*) ใจ [jai]

heaven สวรรค์ [sa-wanj]

heavy, heavily หนัก [nak]

height ความสูง [kwam-soongj]

hell นรก [na-rok]

help ช่วย, ช่วยเหลือ [chuay, chuay leuaj]

here ที่นี่ [thee-nee]

heroin เฮโรอีน [hay-ro-een]

herself เขาเอง [kao ayng]

hide ซ่อน [sawn]

high สูง [soongj]

high school มัธยมศึกษา [mat-tha-yom seuk-saj]

himself เขาเอง [kao ayng]

hire จ้าง [jang]

history ประวัติศาสตร์ [pra-wat-sat]

hit (*bump into*) ชน [chon]; (*fight*) ตอย [toi];
   (*punch, box*) ชก [chok]; (*strike, beat*) ตี [tee]

hold จับ, ถือ [jap, theuj]; (*embrace, hug*) กอด
   [gawt]

hole รู [roo]

holiday วันหยุด [wan yoot]

holy ศักดิ์สิทธิ์ [sak-sit]

home บ้าน [ban]

homeless child เด็กเร่ร่อน [dek ray-rawn]

homesick คิดถึงบ้าน [kit theung ban]

homework การบ้าน [gan-ban]

homosexual (*female*) ทอม, เกย์ [thawm, gay]; (*male*) เกย์ [gay]

honest ซื่อสัตย์ [seu-sat]

honor (*prestige*) เกียรติ [giat]

hook (*for fishing*) เบ็ด [bet]

hope that ... หวังว่า ... [wang wa ...]

horoscope (*consult ~*) ดูดวง [doo duang]

hot (*spicy*) เผ็ด [phet]; (*temperature*) ร้อน [rawn]

house บ้าน [ban]

hug กอด [gawt]

human being มนุษย์ [ma-noot]

humid อบอ้าว [op-ao]

hungry หิวข้าว [hiu kao]

I

idea ความคิด [kwam-kit]

illegal ผิดกฎหมาย [phit got-mai]

impolite ไม่สุภาพ [mai soo-phap]

important สำคัญ [sam-kan]

impossible เป็นไปไม่ได้ [pen pai mai dai]

impressed (by) ประทับใจ [pra-thap-jai]

improve (*make better*) ปรับปรุง [prap-proong]

improved (*better*) ดีขึ้น [dee keun]

in advance ล่วงหน้า [luang na]

in case เผื่อ [pheua]

in order to เพื่อ [pheua]

in style ทันสมัย [than sa-mai]

incense ธูป [thoop]

inch นิ้ว [niu]

include รวม [ruam]

income รายได้ [rai dai]

increase เพิ่ม [pheuhm]; (*enhance*) เสริม [seuhm]

independence อิสรภาพ [eet-sa-ra-phap]

indifferent เฉยๆ [cheuy-cheuy]

industry อุตสาหกรรม [oot-sa-ha-gam]

inflation เงินเฟ้อ [ngeuhn feuh]

information ข้อมูล [kaw-moon]

inner tube ยางใน [yang nai]

innocent บริสุทธิ์ [baw-ree-soot]

insect แมลง [ma-laeng]

insecticide ยาฆ่าแมลง [ya ka ma-laeng]

inspect ตรวจ [truat]

instead (of) แทน, แทนที่ [thaen, thaen thee]

insult (*v*) ดูถูก [doo thook]

insurance (*health*) ประกันสุขภาพ [pra-gan sook-ka-phap]; (*life*) ประกันชีวิต [pra-gan chee-wit]

intelligent ฉลาด [cha-lat]

interest (*bank, loan*) ดอกเบี้ย [dawk bia]

interested (in) สนใจ [son-jai]

interesting น่าสนใจ [na son-jai]

international นานาชาติ [na-na-chat]

interview สัมภาษณ์ [sam-phat]

introduce แนะนำ [nae-nam]

invade บุก, บุกรุก [book, book-rook]

invite ชวน, เชิญ [chuan, cheuhn]

involved (with something) เกี่ยวข้อง [gio kawng]

involves เกี่ยว (กับ) [gio (gap)]

iron (*v*) รีด [reet]

island เกาะ [gaw]

J

jail, in jail ติดคุก [tit kook]

jealous (*envious*) อิจฉา [eet-cha]; (*in love*) หึง [heung]

joke (*v*) พูดเล่น [phoot len]

K

keep เอาไว้ [ao wai]; (*preserve*) รักษา, อนุรักษ์ [rak-sa, a-noo-rak]

keep doing (*continuously*) เรื่อยๆ [reuay-reuay]

key กุญแจ [goon-jae]

kick เตะ [tay]

kill ฆ่า [ka]

kilogram กิโลกรัม, โล [gee-lo-gram, lo]

kilometer กิโลเมตร [gee-lo-met]

kind (*nice*) ใจดี [jai-dee]; (*type*) อย่าง, แบบ [yang, baep]; (*type–formal*) ชนิด, ประเภท [cha-nit, pra-phayt]

king ในหลวง, กษัตริย์ [nai luang, ga-sayt]

kiss (*Thai style*) หอม [hawm]; (*Western style*) จูบ [joop]

kite ว่าว [wao]

know (*~ a person or place*) รู้จัก [roo-jak]; (*general term*) รู้ [roo]; (*polite*) ทราบ [sap]

knowledge ความรู้ [kwam-roo]

L

labor (*n*) แรงงาน [raeng ngan]

lack (*v*) ขาด [kat]

ladder บันได [bun-dai]

lake ทะเลสาบ [tha-lay sap]

land (*piece of land*) ที่ดิน [thee-din]

land measuring unit (1600 sq. meters) ไร่ [rai]

lane (*side street*) ซอย [soi]

language ภาษา [pha-sai]

lantern ตะเกียง [ta-giang]

last (*v*) (*endure*) ทน [thon]; (*adj*) (*final*) สุดท้าย [soot-thai]; (*former, old*) เก่า [gao]

last name นามสกุล [nam sa-goon]

late (*at night*) ดึก [deuk]; (*not on time*) ช้า, ไม่ทัน [cha, mai than]

laugh หัวเราะ [huai-raw]

law กฎหมาย [got-mai]

lazy ขี้เกียจ [kee-giat]

leader ผู้นำ [phoo nam]

learn เรียน, เรียนรู้ [rian, rian roo]

leave ออกไป [awk pai]

left (*leftover*) เหลือ [leuai]; (*side*) ซ้าย [sai]

lend (*let borrow*) ให้ยืม [hai yeum]

let (*allow*) ให้, อนุญาต [hai, a-noo-yat]

let's ... กันเถอะ [... gan theuh]

let go ปล่อย [ploi]

letter จดหมาย [jot-mai]; (*of alphabet*) ตัว [tua]

level (*n*) ระดับ [ra-dap]

library ห้องสมุด [hawng sa-moot]

lick เลีย [lia]

lid ฝา [fai]

lie (*tell a lie*) โกหก [go-hok]

lie down นอน [nawn]

life ชีวิต [chee-wit]

lift (~ *something large*) ยก [yok]; (~ *something small*) หยิบ [yip]

light (*v*) (~ *a fire*) จุด [joot]; (*adj*) (*color*) อ่อน [awn]; (*in weight*) เบา [bao]; (*n*) (*electric*) ไฟ [fai]

like ชอบ [chawp]; (*similar to*) คล้ายๆ [klai-

klai]; (*the same as*) เหมือน [meuang]

like more (*prefer*) ชอบมากกว่า [chawp mak gwa]

like that (*in that way*) **ยังงั้น** [yang-ngan]

like the most ชอบมากที่สุด [chawp mak thee-soot]

like this (*in this way*) ยังงี้ [yang-ngee]

limit, limited จำกัด [jam-gat]

line เส้น [sen]; (*queue*) คิว [kiu]

list (*n*) รายการ [rai-gan]

listen (to) ฟัง [fang]

liter ลิตร [leet]

literature วรรณคดี [wan-na-ka-dee]

litter (*v*) ทิ้งขยะ [thing ka-ya]

little (*amount*) น้อย, นิดหน่อย [noi, nit noi]; (*in size*) เล็ก [lek]

live at อยู่ [yoo]

live with อยู่กับ [yoo gap]

local (*native*) พื้นเมือง [pheun meuang]

lock (*n*) กุญแจ [goon-jae]; (*v*) ล็อก [lawk]

lonely เหงา [ngao]

long (*in time*) นาน [nan]; (*in length*) ยาว [yao]

look (at) ดู [doo]

look down on (*insult*) ดูถูก [doo thook]

look for หา [ha]

looks like ... ดูเหมือน [doo meuang ...]

loose หลวม [luam]

lose (*cause to be lost*) ทำหาย [tham hai]

lose (to) แพ้ [phae]

lose face เสียหน้า [sia na]

lose weight ลดความอ้วน [lot kwam uan]

lose one's way หลงทาง [long thang]

lost (*disappeared, gone*) หาย [hai]

lottery ลอตเตอรี่, หวย [lawt-ta-ree, huay]
lotus flower ดอกบัว [dawk bua]
loud, loudly ดัง [dang]
loud noise เสียงดัง [siang dang]
love (*n*) ความรัก [kwam rak]; (*v*) รัก [rak]
low ต่ำ [tam]
luck โชค [chok]
lucky โชคดี [chok dee]
luxurious ฟุ่มเฟือย [foom-feuay]

M

machine เครื่อง [kreuang]
machinery เครื่องจักร [kreuang jak]
mad (*angry*) โกรธ, โมโห [grot, mo-ho];
(*crazy*) บ้า [ba]
magazine หนังสือ, นิตยสาร [nang-seu,
nit-ta-ya-san]
magic (*n*) ไสยศาสตร์ [sai-ya-sat]
magical วิเศษ [wee-set]
majority ส่วนมาก, ส่วนใหญ่ [suan mak, suan
yai]
make ทำ [tham]; (*cause to happen*) ทำให้
[tham hai]
make a mistake ผิด, ทำผิด [phit, tham phit]
make up one's face แต่งหน้า [taeng na]
man ผู้ชาย [phoo-chai]
manage จัดการ [jat-gan]
manners (*behavior*) นิสัย [nee-sai]; (*etiquette*)
มารยาท [ma-ra-yat]
many มาก, เยอะ, หลาย [mak, yeuh, lai
(*classifier*)]
map แผนที่ [phaen thee]
marijuana กัญชา [gan-cha]

market ตลาด [ta-lat]

marriage license ทะเบียนสมรส [tha-bian somɲ-rot]

married แต่งงานแล้ว [taeng-ngan laeo]

marry แต่งงาน [taeng-ngan]

massage นวด [nuat]

master's degree ปริญญาโท [prin-ya tho]

match (*go together*) เข้ากัน [kao gan]

matches ไม้ขีดไฟ [mai keet fai]

mathematics คณิตศาสตร์ [ka-nit-sat]

maybe บางที [bang-thee]

meaning ความหมาย [kwam-maiɲ]

means that ... หมายความว่า [maiɲ-kwam wa ...]

measure วัด [wat]

medicine ยา [ya]

meet (*have a meeting*) ประชุม [pra-choom]; (*planned*) พบ [phop]; (*unplanned*) เจอ [jeuh]

member สมาชิก [sa-ma-chik]

member of parliament ผู้แทน, ส.ส. [phoo-thaen, sawɲ-sawɲ]

menstruation ประจำเดือน [pra-jam deuan]

message ข้อความ [kaw-kwam]

meter (*metric*) เมตร [met]

method วิธี [wi-thee]

middle กลาง [glang]

might (*v*) อาจจะ [at ja]; (*maybe*) บางที [bang-thee]

mind and heart (*figurative*) ใจ [jai]

mindfulness (*in Buddhism*) สมาธิ [sa-ma-thee]

minister (*government*) รัฐมนตรี [rat-tha-mon-tree]

ministry (*government*) กระทรวง [gra-suang]

minority ส่วนน้อย [suan noi]

minus ลบ [lop]

miss (~ *a person/place*) คิดถึง [kit theung]

missing (*disappeared*) หาย [hai]

mistake, mistaken ผิด [phit]

mistress ไม่น้อย [mia noi]

misunderstand เข้าใจผิด [kao-jai phit]

mix ผสม, รวม [pha-som, ruam]

modern (*new style*) สมัยใหม่ [sa-mai mai];
  (**prosperous**) เจริญ [ja-reuhn]; (*up-to-date*)
  ทันสมัย [than sa-mai]

Mon (*ethnic group*) มอญ [Mawn]

money เงิน [ngeuhn]

mood อารมณ์ [a-rom]

moon พระจันทร์ [phra jan]

moonlight แสงจันทร์ [saeng jan]

more (*add to*) เพิ่ม [pheuhm]; (*again*) อีก [eeg]

mortar (*to pound food*) ครก [krok]

mosquito ยุง [yoong]

mosquito net มุ้ง [moong]

mosquito repellant ยากันยุง [ya gan yoong]

most (*of a number or amount*) ส่วนมาก [suan
  mak]; (*the most*) มากที่สุด [mak thee soot]

mostly ส่วนมาก [suan mak]

mountain ภูเขา [phoo-kao]

move (~ *residence*) ใหญ่ [yai]; (*shift position*)
  เลื่อน [leuan]

movie หนัง, ภาพยนต์ [nang, phap-pha-yon]

movie star ดาราหนัง [da-ra nang]

mud โคลน [klon]

murder (*v*) ฆ่า [ka]; (*n*) ฆาตกรรม [kat-ta-gam]

music ดนตรี [don-tree]; (*songs*) เพลง [phlayng]

musical instrument เครื่องดนตรี [kreuang
  don-tree]

must (*have to*) ต้อง [tawng (*verb*)]; (*strong meaning*) จำต้อง [jam-tawng]

mute person คนใบ้ [kon bai]

myself (*for men*) ผมเอง [phom ayng]; (*for women*) ฉันเอง [chan ayng]

N

nail ตะปู [ta-poo]

naked เปลือย [pleuay]

name ชื่อ [cheu]; (*surname*) นามสกุล [nam sa-goon]

narrow แคบ [kaep]

national แห่งชาติ [haeng chat]

national park อุทยานแห่งชาติ [oot-tha-yan haeng chat]

nationality สัญชาติ [san-chat]

nature, natural ธรรมชาติ [tham-ma-chat]

naughty ดื้อ [deu]

navy กองทัพเรือ [gawng thap reua]

neat, neatly เรียบร้อย [riap-roi]

need (*v*) ต้องการ [tawng-gan]

needle เข็ม [kem]

negotiate เจรจา [jay-ra-ja]

neighbor เพื่อนบ้าน [pheuan ban]

nest รัง [rang]

net (*round fishing* ~) แห [hae]

never (*have* ~) ไม่เคย [mai keuy]

new ใหม่ [mai]

news ข่าว [kao]

newspaper หนังสือพิมพ์ [nang-seu phim]

next ต่อไป [taw pai]

nice (*for person*) ใจดี [jai-dee]

nickname ชื่อเล่น [cheu len]

nightmare ฝันร้าย [fun rai]

no (*that's not right*) ไม่ใช่ [mai chai]

nobody ไม่มีใคร, ไม่มีคน [mai mee krai, mai mee kon]

noise เสียง [siang]

noisy เสียงดัง, หนวกหู [siang dang, nuak hoo]

normal ธรรมดา, ปรกติ [tham-ma-da, pok-ga-tee]

normally (*as usual*) ตามปรกติ [tam pok-ga-tee]

north เหนือ [neua]

northeast ตะวันออกเฉียงเหนือ [ta-wan awk chiang neua]

northwest ตะวันตกเฉียงเหนือ [ta-wan tok chiang neua]

not many/much ไม่มาก [mai mak]

not very ... ไม่ค่อย [mai koi ...]

not yet ยัง, ยังไม่ [yang, yang mai (*verb*)]

notebook สมุด [sa-moot]

nothing ไม่มีอะไร [mai mee a-rai]

nude เปลือย [pleuay]

number (*of house/account*) เลขที่ [lek thee]; (*numeral*) หมายเลข [mai lek]; (*of seat/room*) เบอร์ [beuh]

nursery school อนุบาล [a-noo-ban]

O

obey เชื่อฟัง [cheua fang]

object (*thing*) ของ [kawng]

occupation อาชีพ [a-cheep]

ocean มหาสมุทร [ma-ha sa-moot]; (*sea*) ทะเล [tha-lay]

odor กลิ่น [glin]

offended (*feel ~*) น้อยใจ [noi jai]

official (*formal*) ทางการ [thang-gan]; (*royal*) หลวง [luang]

oil น้ำมัน [nam-mun]; (*for engine*) น้ำมันเครื่อง [nam-mun kreuang]

OK ตกลง [tok-long]

old (*about living things*) แก่ [gae]; (*about objects*) เก่า [gao]; (*very old, ancient*) โบราณ, เก่าแก่ [bo-ran, gao-gae]

old-fashioned (*ancient-style*) โบราณ [bo-ran]; (*out-of-date*) ล้าสมัย [la sa-mai]

on บน, ข้างบน [bon, kang bon]

on time ทัน, ทันเวลา [than, than way-la]

one-way ทางเดียว [thang dio]

only (*a small amount*) แค่, เท่านั้น [kae, thao-nan]; (*one kind*) อย่างเดียว, แต่ [yang-dio, tae]

open เปิด [peuht]

opinion ความคิดเห็น [kwam kit-hen]

opium ฝิ่น [fin]

opportunity โอกาส [o-gat]

orchid ดอกกล้วยไม้ [dawk gluay mai]

order (*v*) สั่ง [sang]

orderly เรียบร้อย [riap-roi]

ordinary ธรรมดา [tham-ma-da]

organization (*agency*) องค์การ [ong-gan]

original (*first*) เดิม [deuhm]; (*of a document*) ต้นฉบับ [ton cha-bap]

other อื่น [(*classifier*) eun]

our(s) ของเรา [kawng rao]

over ข้าม [kam]; (*movie, etc*) จบ, จบแล้ว [jop, jop laeo]

owner (of) เจ้าของ [jao kawng]

P

pack (*~ bags*) เก็บของ [gep kawng]

package (*parcel*) พัสดุ [phat-sa-doo]; (*small, wrapped*) ห่อ [haw]

packet ซอง [sawng]

paddle (*n/v*) พาย [phai]

paid (**already**) จ่ายแล้ว [jai laeo]

paint (*v*) ทาสี [tha see]; (*~ a picture*) วาดรูป, เขียนรูป [wat roop, kian roop]; (*n*) สี, น้ำสี [see, nam see]

painting (*n*) รูปวาด, ภาพวาด [roop-wat, phap-wat]

pair คู่ [koo]

palace พระที่นั่ง [phra-thee-nang]

paper กระดาษ [gra-dat]

papers (*documents*) เอกสาร [ayk-ga-san]

parade แห่ [hae]

park (*v.*) จอด [jawt]; (*n*) (*garden*) สวน [suan]

parliament รัฐสภา [rat-tha-sa-pha]

part (*of something*) ส่วน [suan]; (*region*) ภาค [phak]

participate มีส่วนร่วม [mee suan ruam]

parts (*for vehicle*) อะไหล่ [a-lai]

party งานปาร์ตี้, กินเลี้ยง, งานเลี้ยง [ngan pa-tee, gin liang, ngan liang]; (*political*) พรรคการเมือง [phak gan meuang]

pass (*~ a test*) สอบได้, สอบผ่าน [sawp dai, sawp phan]; (*~ a vehicle*) แซง [saeng]

pass through ผ่าน [phan]

passenger ผู้โดยสาร [phoo doy-san]

past (*n*) อดีต [a-deet]

path ทางเดิน [thang deuhn]

patient (*cool-headed*) ใจเย็น [jai yen];

(*medical*) คนไข้, ผู้ป่วย [kon kai, phoo puay]

pave, paved ลาดยาง [lat yang]

pavilion ศาลา [saj-la]

pawn (*v*) จำนำ [jam-nam]

pay (*v*) จ่าย [jai]

pay attention to เอาใจใส่ [ao jai sai]

pay for (*treat*) เลี้ยง [liang]

pay tax เสียภาษี [siaj pha-seej]

peace สันติภาพ [sunj-tee-phap]

peaceful สงบ [sa-ngop]

peak ยอด [yawt]

peek at แอบดู [aep doo]

peel (*v*) ปลอก [pawk]

pen ปากกา [pak-ga]

pencil ดินสอ [din-sawj]

people คน [kon]; (*common ~*) ชาวบ้าน [chao ban]; (*the ~*) ประชาชน [pra-cha-chon]

percent เปอร์เซ็นต์ [peuh-sen]

perfect สมบูรณ์แบบ [somj-boon baep]

perform แสดง [sa-daeng]

perfume น้ำหอม [nam-hawmj]

period (*grammatical*) จุด [joot]; (*duration*) ช่วง [chuang]; (*in history*) สมัย [sa-maij]

permanent ประจำ, ถาวร [pra-jam, thaj-wawn]

permit (*n*) ใบอนุญาต [bai a-noo-yat]; (*v*) ให้, อนุญาต [hai, a-noo-yat]

person คน [kon]

personal (*affairs, things*) ส่วนตัว [suan tua]

personality บุคลิก [book-ka-lik]

photocopier เครื่องถ่ายเอกสาร [kreuang thai ayk-ga-sanj]

photograph (*n*) รูป, รูปถ่าย [roop, roop thai]; (*v*) ถ่ายรูป [thai roop]

pick up (*a person–come to ~*) มารับ [ma rap];
(*a person–go to ~*) ไปรับ [pai rap]; (*collect*)
เก็บ [gep]; (*~ a large object*) ยก [yok]; (*~ a
small object*) หยิบ [yip]

pickled ดอง [dawng]

picky จู้จี้ [joo-jee]

picture (*drawing*) ภาพวาด [phap wat];
(*photograph*) รูป [roop]

piece ชิ้น [chin]

pill เม็ด [met]

pimp แมงดา [maeng da]

pink สีชมพู [see chom-phoo]

pipe (*for water, gas*) ท่อ [thaw]

pirate โจรสลัด [jon sa-lat]

pity (*v*) สงสาร [song-san]

place ที่, แห่ง, สถานที่ [thee, haeng, sa-than-
thee]

place to stay ที่พัก [thee phak]

plan (*n*) แผน [phaen]; (*v*) วางแผน [wang
phaen]

planet ดาว [dao]

plant (*n*) ต้นไม้ [ton-mai]; (*v*) ปลูก [plook]

play (*n*) (*drama*) ละคร [la-kawn]; (*v*) เล่น
[len]

please (*formal*) กรุณา, โปรด [ga-roo-na, prot];
(*informal*) ช่วย [chuay (*v*)]

plow (*v*) ไถ [thai]

pocket กระเป๋า [gra-pao]

point (*~ of land*) แหลม [laem]; (*physical, in
discussion*) จุด [joot]; (*score*) คะแนน [ka-
naen]; (*v*) (*~ at*) ชี้ [chee]

pointed แหลม [laem]

poison (*n*) ยาพิษ [ya phit]

poisonous มีพิษ [mee phit]

policy นโยบาย [na-yo-bai]

polite, politely สุภาพ [soo-phap]

political party พรรคการเมือง [phak gan meuang]

politics การเมือง [gan meuang]

polluted เสีย, เป็นพิษ [siaj, pen phit]

poor จน [jon]

popular นิยม [nee-yom]

population พลเมือง, ประชากร [phon-la-meuang, pra-cha-gawn]

pornographic โป๊ [po]

possessions ของ, ข้าวของ [kawngj, kao-kawngj]

postpone เลื่อนเวลา [leuan way-la]

pour water on รดน้ำ [rot nam]

powder แป้ง [paeng]

power (*authority*) อำนาจ [am-nat]; (*force*) กำลัง [gam-lang]; (*influence*) อิทธิพล [it-thee-phon]; (*strength*) แรง [raeng]

practice (*v*) ซ้อม [sawm]

pray (*make wish, vow*) อธิฐาน [a-theet-thanj]

prefer ชอบมากกว่า [chawp mak gwa]

pregnant มีท้อง [mee thawng]

prepare (*get ready*) เตรียม, เตรียมตัว [triam, triam tua]

prepared (*ready*) พร้อมแล้ว, เรียบร้อย [phrawm laeo, riap-roi]

present (*n*) (*gift*) ของฝาก [kawngj-kwanj]; (*adj*) (*the ~ time*) ปัจจุบัน [pat-joo-ban]; (*v*) (*to offer*) เสนอ [sa-neuhj]

preserve รักษา, อนุรักษ์ [rak-saj, a-noo-rak]

president ประธานาธิบดี [pra-tha-na thi-baw-dee]

press down on กด, บีบ [got, beep]

pretend ทำตัว [tham tua]

pretty งาม [ngam]

price ราคา [ra-ka]

primary school ประถม [pra-thom˩]

prime minister นายกรัฐมนตรี [na-yok rat-tha-mon-tree]

prince เจ้าชาย [jao chai]

princess เจ้าหญิง [jao ying˩]

prison คุก [kook]

prisoner นักโทษ [nak thot]

private (*company*) เอกชน [ayk-ga-chon];
  (*personal*) ส่วนตัว [suan tua]

probably คงจะ [kong ja (*v*)]

problem ปัญหา [pan-ha˩]; (*matter*) เรื่อง [reuang]

procession แห่ [hae]

produce (*v*) (*manufacture*) ผลิต [pha-lit]

profession อาชีพ [a-cheep]

program รายการ [rai-gan]

prohibit ห้าม [ham]

project โครงการ [krong-gan]

promise (*v*) สัญญา [sun˩-ya]

promote ส่งเสริม [song-seuhm˩]

propose (*offer*) เสนอ [sa-neuh˩]

protect ป้องกัน [pawng-gan]

proud ภูมิใจ [phoom-jai]

prove พิสูจน์ [phee-soot]

public (*adj*) สาธารณะ [sa˩-tha-ra-na]

pull ดึง [deung]

punish ทำโทษ [tham thot]

pure บริสุทธิ์ [baw-ree-soot]

purple สีม่วง [see˩ muang]

purse กระเป๋า [gra-pao˩]

push (~ *door, etc*) ผลัก [phlak]; (*press down on*) กด, บีบ [got, beep]

put away เก็บไว้ [gep wai]

put down วาง [wang]

put forth ออก [awk]

put in ใส่ [sai]

put in (*add to*) เติม [teuhm]

put on clothes ใส่เสื้อผ้า [sai seua-pha]

put on make-up แต่งหน้า [taeng na]

put out (~ *fire/lights*) ดับ [dap]

put together (*combine*) รวม [ruam]

Q

quality คุณภาพ [koon-na-phap]

quantity จำนวน [jam-nuan]

queen ราชินี [ra-chee-nee]

question (*n*) คำถาม [kam thamŋ]

queue (*n*) คิว [kiu]

quick, quickly เร็ว, เร็วๆ [reo, reo-reo]

quiet เงียบ [ngiap]

quit (~ *a job*) ลาออก [la awk]; (*stop*) เลิก [leuhk]

R

race (*v*) แข่ง, แข่งขัน [kaeng, kaeng-kunŋ]

radio วิทยุ [wit-tha-yoo]

rafting ล่องแพ [lawng phae]

raise (*bring up*) เลี้ยง [liang]

rape (*v*) ข่มขืน [kom keunŋ]

rare หายาก [haŋ yak]

rate (*n*) อัตรา [at-tra]

rather (~ *do something*) ดีกว่า [(*verb*) dee gwa]

raw ดิบ [dip]

razor มีดโกน [meet gon]

razor blade ใบมีด [bai meet]

read อ่าน [an]; (*as an activity*) อ่านหนังสือ [an nang-seu]

read it to me อ่านให้ฟัง [an hai fang]

ready (*finished*) เสร็จแล้ว [set laeo]; (*prepared*) เรียบร้อย, พร้อม [riap-roi, phrawm]

real แท้ [thae]

reason (*n*) เหตุผล [hayt-phon]

receipt ใบเสร็จ [bai set]

receive ได้, ได้รับ [dai, dai rap]

recommend แนะนำ [nae-nam]

red สีแดง [see daeng]

reduce ลด [lot]

reduce weight ลดความอ้วน [lot kwam uan]

refugee ผู้อพยพ [phoo op-pha-yop]

refugee camp ศูนย์อพยพ [soon op-pha-yop]

register (*v*) จดทะเบียน [jot tha-bian]

regular (*as always*) ประจำ [pra-jam]; (*ordinary*) ธรรมดา [tham-ma-da]

regulation ระเบียบ [ra-biap]

relative(s) ญาติ [yat]

release ปล่อย [ploi]

remember จำ [jam]

rent (*v*) เช่า [chao]; (*charter entire vehicle for a group*) เหมา [mao]

rent to someone, for rent ให้เช่า [hai chao]

repair ซ่อม [sawm]

reply (*v*) ตอบ [tawp]

report (*n/v*) รายงาน [rai-ngan]

representative ผู้แทน [phoo-thaen]

require ต้องการ [tawng-gan]

research (*v*) วิจัย [wee-jai]

resemble ดูเหมือน [doo meuang]

reserve (*v*) จอง [jawng]

respect (*believe in*) นับถือ [nap-theu]; (*in society*) เคารพ [kao-rop]

respond ตอบ [tawp]

responsible (for) รับผิดชอบ [rap-phit-chawp]

rest (*v*) (*relax*) พักผ่อน [phak-phawn]; (*n*) (*the ~, leftover*) ที่เหลือ [thee leua]

restroom ห้องน้ำ [hawng nam]

results ผล [phon]

return (*come back*) กลับมา [glap ma]; (*give back*) คืน [keun]; (*go back*) กลับไป [glap pai]

revenge (*v*) แก้แค้น [gae kaen]

revolution (*political*) การปฏิวัติ [gan pa-tee-wat]

revolve หมุน [moon]

rhythm จังหวะ [jang-wa]

rice ข้าว [kao]

rich (*wealthy*) รวย [ruay]

rich person เศรษฐี [sayt-thee]

ride ขี่ [kee]

right (*correct*) ถูก, ถูกต้อง [thook, thook-tawng]; (*side*) ขวา [kwa]

rights สิทธิ์ [sit]

rise ขึ้น [keun]

river แม่น้ำ [mae-nam]

road (*street*) ถนน [tha-non]; (*way, route*) ทาง [thang]

rob ปล้น, ขโมย [plon, ka-moy]

rock หิน [hin]

rocket จรวด [ja-ruat]

rope เชือก [cheuak]

rose ดอกกุหลาบ [dawk goo-lap]

rotate หมุน [moon]

rotten เน่า [nao]

round (*adj*) (*circular*) กลม [glom]; (*n*) (*in boxing*) ยก [yok]

royal หลวง [luang]

rubber ยาง [yang]

rubber tree ต้นยาง [ton yang]

ruins เมืองเก่า [meuang gao]

rule (*regulation*) ระเบียบ [ra-biap]

ruler (*for measuring*) ไม้บรรทัด [mai ban-that]

rumor ข่าวลือ [kao-leu]

run วิ่ง [wing]

run away หนี [nee]

run into (*crash*) ชน [chon]; (*meet*) เจอ [jeuh]

run over เหยียบ [yiap]

S

sacred ศักดิ์สิทธิ์ [sak-sit]

safe (*adj*) ปลอดภัย [plawt-phai]

said that ... พูดว่า [phoot wa ...]

sailboat เรือใบ [reua bai]

sailor ทหารเรือ [tha-han reua]

salary เงินเดือน [ngeuhn deuan]

salted, salty เค็ม [kem]

same (*equal to each other*) เท่ากัน [thao-gan]; (*one and the ~*) เดียวกัน [(*classifier*) dio-gan]

same as (*characteristics*) เหมือน [meuan]

same as before เหมือนเดิม [meuan deuhm]

same as each other เหมือนกัน [meuan-gan]

sand ทราย [sai]

sanitary napkin ผ้าอนามัย [pha a-na-mai]

sarong โสร่ง [sa-rong]

satellite ดาวเทียม [dao thiam]

satisfied พอใจ [phaw-jai]

save เก็บไว้ [gep wai]; (~ *money*) เก็บเงิน [gep ngeuhn]

saw (*n/v*) (*tool*) เลื่อย [leuay]

say พูด [phoot]

say that ... พูดว่า [phoot wa ...]

scale (*for weighing*) ชั่ง [chang]

scent กลิ่น [glin]

schedule (*n*) ตารางเวลา [ta-rang way-la]

scholarship ทุน [thoon]

school โรงเรียน [rong-rian]

science วิทยาศาสตร์ [wit-tha-ya-sat]

scissors กรรไกร [gun-grai]

scold (*reprimand*) ดุ [doo]; (*strongly*) ด่า [da]

score (*n*) คะแนน [ka-naen]

screwdriver ไขควง [kai kuang]

sea ทะเล [tha-lay]

seat ที่นั่ง [thee-nang]

second (*in time*) วินาที [wee na-thee]; (*number two*) ที่สอง [thee sawng]

secondary school มัธยมศึกษา [mat-tha-yom seuk-sa]

secondhand (*used*) มือสอง, ใช้แล้ว [meu sawng, chai laeo]

see เห็น [hen]

see a movie ดูหนัง [doo nang]

seed เม็ด [met]

seems like ดูเหมือน [doo meuan]

selfish, self-centered เห็นแก่ตัว [hen gae tua]

sell ขาย [kai]; (*engage in trade*) ขายของ, ค้าขาย [kai kawng, ka kai]

send ส่ง [song]

sensitive (*easily offended*) ใจน้อย [jai noi]

sentence (*grammatical*) ประโยค [pra-yok]

separate (*v*) แยก [yaek]

separately แตกหัก [tang hak]

serious (*earnest*) จริงจัง [jing-jang]; (*tense*) เครียด [kriat]

serve, service บริการ [baw-ree-gan]

set (*n*) ชุด [choot]

set up ตั้ง [tang]

sew เย็บ [yep]; (*make clothes*) ตัดเสื้อ [tat seua]

sex (*gender*) เพศ [phet]; (*have ~*) มีเซ็กซ์ [mee sek]

shade ร่ม [rom]

shadow เงา [ngao]

shake hands จับมือ [jap meu]

shampoo (*n*) ยาสระผม [ya sa phomj]

share (*divide up*) แบ่ง [baeng]; (*use together*) ใช้ร่วมกัน [chai ruam gan]

sharp คม [kom]

shave โกนหนวด [gon nuat]

shell, shellfish หอย [hoij]

ship (*n*) เรือ [reua]

shoot ยิง [ying]; (*~ a gun*) ยิงปืน [ying peun]

shop (*n*) ร้าน [ran]; (*v*) ซื้อของ [seu kawngj]

shore ฝั่งทะเล [fang tha-lay]

short (*in height*) เตี้ย [tia]; (*in length*) สั้น [sun]

should น่าจะ, ควรจะ [na ja (*v*), kuan ja (*v*)]; (*have to, must*) ต้อง [tawng (*v*)]

shout (*v*) ร้อง [rawng]

show (*n*) การแสดง, โชว์ [gan sa-daeng, cho]; (*v*) แสดง [sa-daeng]

shrink หด [hot]

shy อาย, ขี้อาย [ai, kee ai]

Siam สยาม [Sa-yamj]

side ข้าง [kang]

sight (*eyesight*) สายตา [saiɲ ta]

sign (*signboard*) ป้าย [paî]

sign language ภาษามือ [pha-saɲ meu]

sign one's name เซ็นชื่อ [sen cheu]

signal สัญญาณ [suɲ-yan]

similar to ... คล้ายๆ [klai-klai ...]

similar to each other คล้ายๆกัน [klai-klai gan]

sin บาป [bap]

since ตั้งแต่ [tang-tae]

sincere จริงใจ [jing-jai]

sing ร้องเพลง [rawng phlayng]

single (*only one*) เดี่ยว [(*classifier*) dio]; (*unmarried*) โสด [sot]

sink (*a boat sinking*) เรือล่ม [reua lom]; (*drown*) จมน้ำ [jom-nam]

sit นั่ง [nang]

size (*clothing*) ไซส์ [sai]; (*extent*) ขนาด [ka-nat]

skill ความสามารถ [kwam sa-mat]

skin (*n*) ผิว [phiuɲ]; (*hide*) หนัง [nangɲ]

sky ฟ้า [fa]

slang สแลง [sa-laeng]

slave ทาส [that]

sleep (*is sleeping*) หลับ, นอนหลับ [lap, nawn lap]; (*lie down*) นอน [nawn]

sleepy ง่วงนอน [nguang nawn]

slice หั่น, ซอย [hun, soi]

slip, slippery ลื่น [leun]

slow, slowly ช้า, ช้าๆ [cha, cha-cha]

small เล็ก [lek]

smart (*intelligent*) ฉลาด [cha-lat]

smell (*n*) กลิ่น [glin]; (*v*) ดม [dom]

smells bad เหม็น [men]

smells good หอม [hawm]

smile ยิ้ม [yim]

smoke (*n*) ควัน [kwan]; (*from a fire*) ควันไฟ [kwan fai]

smoke cigarettes สูบบุหรี่ [soop boo-ree]

smooth เรียบ [riap]

smuggle ลักลอบขน [lap lawp kon]

snack (*n*) ขนม [ka-nom]; (*v*) กินเล่น [gin len]

sneeze จาม [jam]

snore กรน [gron]

so (*therefore*) เลย, ก็เลย [leuy, gaw leuy]

so that (*in order to*) เพื่อ [pheua]

soap สบู่ [sa-boo]

society สังคม [sang-kom]

soft (*for sounds*) เบา [bao]; (*gentle*) อ่อน [awn]; (*spongy, tender*) นุ่ม [noom]; (*yielding*) นิ่ม [nim]

software ซอฟท์แวร์ [sawf-wae]

soil (*n*) ดิน [din]

solve แก้ไข [gae kai]

some (*things, etc*) บาง [bang (*classifier*)]

some, somewhat บ้าง [bang]

song(s) เพลง [phlayng]

sorry (*excuse me*) ขอโทษ [kaw-thot]; (*unhappy*) เสียใจ [siaj-jai]

sound เสียง [siang]

sour เปรี้ยว [prio]

south ใต้ [tai]

southeast ตะวันออกเฉียงใต้ [ta-wan awk chiang tai]

southwest ตะวันตกเฉียงใต้ [ta-wan tok chiang tai]

space (*outer~*) อวกาศ [a-wa-gat]; (*place*) ที่ [thee]

spacious กว้าง [gwang]

spark plug หัวเทียน [hua thian]

speak พูด [phoot]; (*converse*) คุย [kui]

speaker (*loudspeaker*) ลำโพง [lum-phong]

special, specially พิเศษ [phee-set]

speed ความเร็ว [kwam-reo]

spell (*v*) สะกด [sa-got]

spend money ใช้เงิน [chai ngeuhn]

spirit วิญญาณ [win-yan]; (*in body*) ขวัญ
   [kwan]; (*will-power*) กำลังใจ [gam-lang jai]

spit (*saliva*) น้ำลาย [nam-lai]

spit out ถุย [thui]

spoiled (~ *food*) เสีย [sia]

sponsor (*v*) สนับสนุน [sa-nap sa-noon]

spray ฉีด [cheet]

spread on ทา [tha]

squeeze บีบ [beep]

stage (*n*) เวที [way-thee]

stand (*v*) ยืน [yeun]

stand up ลุกขึ้น [look keun]

star ดาว [dao]

stare (at) จ้อง [jawng]

start (*v*) เริ่ม [reuhm]

starve อด, อดข้าว [ot, ot kao]

state (*n*) (*as in United States*) รัฐ [rat];
   (*condition*) สภาพ [sa-phap]

station สถานที่ [sa-tha-nee]

statue รูปปั้น [roop pun]

status ฐานะ [tha-na]

stay พัก [phak]

stay at home อยู่บ้าน [yoo ban]

stay overnight ค้างคืน [kang keun]

steal ขโมย [ka-moy]

step on เหยียบ [yiap]

stick (*wood*) ไม้ [mai]

stick to ติด [tit]

sticky [nioj]

still (*yet*) ยัง [yang]

sting (*v*) ต่อย [toi]

stingy ขี้เหนียว [kee nioj]; (*greedy*) งก [ngok]

stolen หาย [haij]

stone (*n*) หิน [hinj]

stop หยุด [yoot]; (*quit*) เลิก [leuhk]; (~ *a vehicle*) จอด [jawt]

story (*fable*) นิทาน [nee-than]; (*floor*) ชั้น [chan]; (*matter, problem*) เรื่อง [reuang]; (*a ~ to tell*) เรื่องราว [reuang laoj]

straight ตรง [trong]

strange แปลก [plaek]

stream ห้วย [huay]

street ถนน [tha-nonj]; (*side ~, lane*) ซอย [soi]

stretch ยืด [yeut]

strict (*rigid, austere*) เข้มงวด [kem nguat]

string (*rope*) เชือก [cheuak]; (*thread*) ด้าย [dai]

striped ลาย [lai]

strong แข็งแรง [kaengj-raeng]

stubborn ดื้อ [deu]

student นักเรียน [nak rian]; (*high level*) นักศึกษา [nak seuk-saj]; (~ *of someone*) ลูกศิษย์ [look-sit]

study เรียน [rian]; (*at high level*) ศึกษา [seuk-saj]; (*go to school*) เรียนหนังสือ [rian nangj-seuj]

stupid โง่ [ngo]

style แบบ [baep]; (*for hair*) ทรง [song]

stylish ทันสมัย [than sa-mai]

subject (*in school*) วิชา [wee-cha]; (*topic*) เรื่อง [reuang]

substitute (*v*) แทน [thaen]

suburb(s) ชานเมือง [chan meuang]

succeed (*finish*) สำเร็จ [sam-ret]; (*get results*) ได้ผล [dai phon]

suck ดูด [doot]; (*keep in mouth*) อม [om]; (*pump*) สูบ [soop]

suffer ทรมาน [thaw-ra-man]

suicide, commit suicide (*v*) ฆ่าตัวตาย [ka tua tai]

suitcase กระเป๋า [gra-pao]

sun พระอาทิตย์ [phra a-thit]

sunbathe อาบแดด [ab-daet]

sunburn ผิวไหม้ [phiw mai]

sunflower ทานตะวัน [than ta-wan]

sunrise พระอาทิตย์ขึ้น [phra a-thit keun]

sunset พระอาทิตย์ตก [phra a-thit tok]

suntan lotion ครีมกันแดด [keem gan daet]

superstition โชคลาง [chok lang]

supervise คุม [koom]

support (*v*) สนับสนุน [sa-nap sa-noon]

suppose that ... สมมติว่า [som-moot wa ...]

sure (*certain, surely*) แน่ใจ, แน่นอน [nae-jai, nae nawn]; (*confident*) มั่นใจ [mun-jai]

surprised ประหลาดใจ [pra-lat jai]; (*startled*) ตกใจ [tok-jai]

surrender ยอมแพ้ [yawm phae]

surround รอบ [rawp]

suspect (*v*) สงสัย [song-sai]

suspect that ... สงสัยว่า [song-sai wa ...]

swamp บึง, หนอง [beung, nawng]

sweat (*n*) เหงื่อ [ngeua]; (*v*) เหงื่อออก [ngeua awk]

sweep กวาด [gwat]

sweet หวาน [wan]; (*personality*) อ่อนหวาน [awn wan]

swim ว่ายน้ำ [wai-nam]

swimming pool สระว่ายน้ำ [sa wai-nam]

sword ดาบ [dap]

sympathize (with) เห็นใจ [hen-jai]

symptom อาการ [a-gan]

system ระบบ [ra-bop]

T

tail หาง [hang]

take (*something away*) เอาไป [ao pai]; (*want*) เอา [ao]

take a bath อาบน้ำ [ab-nam]

take a picture ถ่ายรูป [thai roop]

take a trip ไปเที่ยว [pai thio]

take a walk เดินเล่น [deuhn len]

take advantage of เอาเปรียบ [ao priap]

take care of ดูแล [doo-lae]

take medicine กินยา [gin ya]

take off clothes ถอดเสื้อผ้า [thawt seua-pha]

take off shoes ถอดรองเท้า [thawt rawng-thao]

talented มีพรสวรรค์ [mee phawn sa-wan]

talk (*converse*) คุย [kui]; (*say, speak*) พูด [phoot]

tall สูง [soong]

taste (*n*) (*in styles*) รสนิยม [rot-sa-nee-yom]; (*flavor*) รส, รสชาติ [rot, rot chat]; (*v*) ชิม [chim]

tattoo (*n*) รอยสัก [roi sak]; (*v*) สัก [sak]

tax (*n*) ภาษี [pha-see]

teach สอน [sawn]

tear (*n*) (*from crying*) น้ำตา [nam ta]; (*v*) ขาด [kat]

tear down ทุบทิ้ง [thoop thing]

tease (*v*) ล้อเล่น [law len]; (*flirtatiously*) แซว [saeo]

technical school เทคนิค [thek-nik]

teenager วัยรุ่น [wai-roon]

television โทรทัศน์ [tho-ra-that]

tell บอก [bawk]

tell that ... บอกว่า [bawk wa ...]

temperature อุณหภูมิ [oon-ha-phoom]

temporary, temporarily ชั่วคราว [chua-krao]

term (*semester*) เทอม [theuhm]

terrible แย่ [yae]

test (*v*) (*take a ~*) สอบ [sawp]

that (*a thing*) นั่น [nan]; (*as in* "I think ~") ว่า [wa]; (*as in* "~ shirt") นั้น [(*classifier*) nan]; (*as in* "the shop ~") ที่ [thee]

their(s) ของเขา [kawng kao]

then (*at that time*) ตอนนั้น [tawn-nan]

then ... (*two actions*) แล้วก็ [laeo gaw ...]

there (*over ~*) ที่นั่น [thee-nan]; (*way over ~*) ที่โน่น [thee-noon]

there is มี [mee]

there isn't ไม่มี [mai mee]

therefore เลย, ก็เลย [leuy, gaw leuy]

thick (*concentrated*) ข้น [kon]; (*in width*) หนา [na]

thief โจร, ขโมย [jon, ka-moy]

thin (*for objects*) บาง [bang]; (*for people*) ผอม [phawm]

thing(s) ของ [kawng]

think คิด [kit]

think that ... คิดว่า [kit wa ...]

thirsty หิวน้ำ [hiw nam]

this (*a thing*) นี่ [nee]; (*as in* "~ shirt") นี้ [(*classifier*) nee]

this is ... นี่คือ [nee keu ...]

this kind ยังงี้, แบบนี้ [yang-ngee, baep nee]

this way (*like this*) ยังงี้ [yang-ngee]; (*this route*) ทั้งนี้ [thang nee]

thread (*n*) ด้าย [dai]

through (*finished*) เสร็จแล้ว [set laeo]; (*go* ~) ผ่าน [phan]

throw (*forcefully*) **ขว้าง** [kwang]; (*toss*) โยน [yon]

throw away ทิ้ง [thing]

tickles, it tickles จั๊กกะจี้ [jak-ga-jee]

tie (*v*) ผูก, มัด [phook, mut]

tight, tightly สนิท [sa-nit]

tight-fitting คับ, ฟิต [kap, fit]

time เวลา [way-la]

timetable ตารางเวลา [ta-rang way-la]

tire (*for vehicle*) ยาง, ยางรถ [yang, yang rot]; (*flat*~) ยางแบน [yang baen]; (*leaking* ~) ยางรั่ว [yang rua]

tired (*mentally, physically*) เหนื่อย [neuay]; (*sore, stiff*) เมื่อย [meuay]

to (*in order* ~) เพื่อ [pheua]

together (*do something* ~) ด้วยกัน [duay-gan]; (*gather* ~) รวม [ruam]

toilet ห้องน้ำ [hawng nam]

told (*v*) บอกแล้ว [bawk laeo]

told someone that ... บอกว่า [bawk wa ...]

ton ตัน [tun]

tone (*in Thai*) ระดับเสียง [ra-dap siang]

too (*also*) ด้วย [duay]; (*the same*) เหมือนกัน [meuan-gan]; (*together*) ด้วยกัน [duay-gan]; (*adj*) (*as in "~ hot"*) ไป, เกินไป [pai, geuhn pai]

tool เครื่องมือ [kreuang meu]

tooth ฟัน [fun]; (*false ~*) ฟันปลอม [fun plawm]

toothbrush แปรงสีฟัน [praeng see fun]

toothpaste ยาสีฟัน [ya see fun]

toothpick ไม้จิ้มฟัน [mai jim fun]

torn ขาด [kat]

touch (*actively*) จับ, ถูก [jap, thook]; (*come in contact*) โดน, ถูก [don, thook]

tough (*meat, etc*) เหนียว [nio]

tourism การท่องเที่ยว [gan thawng-thio]

tourist นักท่องเที่ยว [nak thawng-thio]

toward ต่อ [taw]

town เมือง [meuang]

toy ของเล่น [kawng len]

trade (*n*) (*commerce*) การค้า [gan ka]; (*v*) (*swap*) แลก [laek]

trademark เครื่องหมาย [kreuang mai]

tradition (*culture*) วัฒนธรรม [wat-tha-na-tham]; (*custom*) ประเพณี [pra-phay-nee]

traditional (*old-style*) สมัยเก่า [sa-mai gao]; (*original*) เดิม [deuhm]

traffic จราจร [ja-ra-jawn]

traffic jam รถติด [rot tit]

train (*v*) ฝึก [feuk]; (*n*) รถไฟ [rot-fai]

transfer โอน [on]

translate แปล [plae]

transvestite เกย์, กะเทย [gay, ga-theuy]

trash ขยะ [ka-ya]

travel (*v*) เดินทาง [deuhn-thang]

treat (*v*) (*medical*) รักษา [rak-sa͞a]; (*pay for*)
   เลี้ยง [liang]

tree ต้นไม้ [toᶥn mai]

tribe เผ่า [pha͗o]

trick (*do bad things*) แกล้ง [glaeng]

trophy ถ้วย [thuay]

trouble (*be in ~*) เดือดร้อน [deuat-rawn];
   (*have problem*) มีปัญหา [mee paᶥn-ha͞a]

true จริง [jing]; (*really*) จริงๆ [jing-jing]

trust (*v*) ไว้ใจ [wai-jai]

try (*make an effort*) พยายาม [pha͗-ya-yam];
   (*taste*) ชิม [chiᶥm]; (*test out*) ลอง [lawng]

try on ลองใส่ [lawng sa͞i]

tube หลอด [lawt]

turn (*~ a corner*) เลี้ยว [lio]; (*revolve*) หมุน
   [mooᶥng]; (*twist*) บิด [biᶥt]

turn down (*~ volume*) ค่อย [koᶥi]

turn off (*close*) ปิด [piᶥt]

turn off lights ปิดไฟ [piᶥt faᶥi]

turn on (*open*) เปิด [peuht]

turn on lights เปิดไฟ [peuht faᶥi]

turn up (*~ volume*) ขึ้น [keuᶥn]

twice สองครั้ง [sawng krang]

twins ลูกแฝด [look faet]

type (*v*) พิมพ์ดีด [phim deet]; (*n*) (*kind*) อย่าง,
   แบบ [yang, baep]; (*kind–formal*) ชนิด,
   ประเภท [cha-niᶥt, pra͗-phayt]

U

ugly น่าเกลียด [na͞a gliat]

umbrella ร่ม [romᶥ]

under (*~ an area*) ล่าง, ข้างล่าง [lang, kang
   lang]; (*~ an object*) ใต้ [tai]

understand เข้าใจ [kao-jai]

undo แก้ [gae]

undress ถอดเสื้อผ้า [thawt seua-pha]

unemployed ตกงาน [tok ngan]

unfriendly ไม่เป็นมิตร [mai pen mit]

unhappy เสียใจ [siaŋ-jai]; (*lost something*)
เสียดาย [siaŋ-dai]

uniform ชุด, เครื่องแบบ [choot, kreuang baep]

United Nations สหประชาชาติ [Sa-ha Pra-cha-
chat]

universal สากล [saŋ-gon]

universe จักรวาล [jak-gra-wan]

university มหาวิทยาลัย [ma-haŋ-wit-tha-ya-lai]

unless ... นอกจากว่า [nawk-jak wa ...]

unlucky ซวย, โชคไม่ดี, โชคร้าย [suay, chok
mai dee, chok rai]

unmarried โสด [sot]

untie แก้ [gae]

up ขึ้น [keun]

upset (*feeling*) ไม่สบายใจ [mai sa-bai jai]

urinate (colloq.) เยี่ยว [yio]

use (*v*) ใช้ [chai]

used (*secondhand*) ใช้แล้ว, มือสอง [chai laeo,
meu sawngŋ]

used to (*accustomed to*) ชิน [chin]; (*did in the
past*) เคย [keuy]

used up หมด [mot]

useful มีประโยชน์ [mee pra-yot]

usual (*regular, ordinary*) ธรรมดา [tham-ma-da]

usually (*normally*) ปกติ [pok-ga-tee]; (*ordinar-
ily*) ธรรมดา [tham-ma-da]; (*mostly*) ส่วนมาก
[suan mak]

V

vacation (*from school*) พักเรียน [phak rian];
   (*from work*) พักร้อน [phak rawn]

valuable มีค่า [mee ka]

value ค่า, ราคา [ka, ra-ka]

various ต่างๆ [tang-tang]

vehicle รถ [rot]

very มาก [mak]

view วิว [wiu]

village หมู่บ้าน [moo-ban]

violent รุนแรง [roon-raeng]

violin ซอ [saw]

visa วีซ่า [wee-sa]

visit (*~ a person*) ไปหา, เยี่ยม [pai ha, yiam];
   (*~ a place*) ไปเที่ยว [pai thio]; (*stop by, drop
   by*) แวะ [wae]

vitamin วิตามิน [wit-ta-min]

vocabulary คำศัพท์ [kam sap]

voice เสียง [siang]

volcano ภูเขาไฟ [phoo-kao fai]

volunteer (*n*) ผู้อาสาสมัคร [phoo a-sa-sa-mak];
   (*v*) อาสา, อาสาสมัคร [a-sa, a-sa-sa-mak]

vote (for) เลือก [leuak]

vowel สระ [sa-ra]

W

wage ค่าจ้าง [ka jang]

wait (for) คอย, รอ [koi, raw]

wake up ตื่น, ตื่นนอน [teun, teun nawn]; (*~
   another person*) ปลุก [plook]

walk เดิน [deuhn]

wall (*of a city/garden*) กำแพง [gam-phaeng]

want เอา [ao]; (*would like, need*) ต้องการ [tawng-gan]

want to (*~ do something*) อยาก, ต้องการ [yak, tawng-gan]

war สงคราม [song-kram]

warehouse โกดัง [go-dang]

warm (*temperature*) อุ่น [oon]; (*feeling*) อบอุ่น [op-oon]

warn เตือน [teuan]

wash ล้าง [lang]

wash clothes ซักเสื้อผ้า [sak seua-pha]

wash dishes ล้างจาน [lang jan]

wash one's face ล้างหน้า [lang na]

wash one's hair สระผม [sa phom]

waste (*v*) เสีย [sia]

watch (*n*) นาฬิกา [na-lee-ga]; (*v*) ดู [doo]

water น้ำ [nam]

waterfall น้ำตก [nam-tok]

wave (*n*) คลื่น [kleun]

way (*method, means*) วิธี, วิธีการ [wi-thee, wi-thee-gan]; (*route*) ทาง [thang]

weak (*feeling*) อ่อนแอ, ไม่มีแรง [awn-ae, mai mee raeng]; (*~ tea, etc*) อ่อน [awn]

wealthy รวย [ruay]

weapon อาวุธ [a-woot]

wear ใส่ [sai]

wedding งานแต่งงาน [ngan taeng-ngan]

weigh ชั่ง [chang]

weight น้ำหนัก [nam-nak]

welcome (*formal phrase*) ยินดีต้อนรับ [yin dee tawn rap]

well (*expertly*) เก่ง [geng]; (*fine*) สบายดี [sa-bai dee]; (*n*) (*for water*) บ่อ [baw]

well-mannered เรียบร้อย [riap-roi]

west, western ตะวันตก [ta-wan tok]

wet เปียก [piak]

wheat ข้าวสาลี [kao saj-lee]

wheel ล้อ [law]

whether (or not) … ไม่ว่า.. [mai wa …]

who (*as in* "the person who …") ที่ [thee]

whisper กระซิบ [gra-sip]

whistle (*v*) ผิวปาก [phiw pak]

white สีขาว [see kao]

wide กว้าง [gwang]

will, would (*v*) จะ [ja]

will-power กำลังใจ [gam-lang jai]

win (*beat*) ชนะ [cha-na]

wipe เช็ด [chet]

wire ลวด [luat]; (*electrical*) สายไฟ [sai fai]

wish (*v*) ปรารถนา [prat-tha-na]

without (*not having*) ไม่มี [mai mee]

woman ผู้หญิง [phoo-ying]

wonder if … สงสัยว่า [song-sai wa …]

wonderful แจ๋ว, เยี่ยม [jaeo, yiam]

wood ไม้ [mai]

word คำ [kam]

work (*n*) งาน [ngan]; (*v*) ทำงาน [tham-ngan]

world โลก [lok]

worry, worried เป็นห่วง [pen huang]

worth (*value*) ค่า, ราคา [ka, ra-ka]

worth it, worthwhile คุ้ม, คุ้มค่า [koom, koom ka]

would, will (*v*) จะ [ja]

would be better to … ดีกว่า [(*verb*) dee gwa]

would like (to) ต้องการ [tawng-gan]

wrap (~ *a package*) ห่อ [haw]

write เขียน [kian]
wrong, wrongly ผิด, ไม่ถูก [phit, mai thook]

X

xylophone ระนาด [ra-nat]

Y

yellow สีเหลือง [see leuang]
yes (*polite–female*) ค่ะ [ka]; (*polite–male*) ครับ
  [krup]; (*that's right*) ใช่ [chai]
yet (*still*) ยัง [yang]
young อ่อน [awn]
yourself คุณเอง [koon ayng]

Z

zero ศูนย์ [soon]
zoo สวนสัตว์ [suan sat]
zone เขต [kayt]

PHRASEBOOK

Note: Phrases are marked (*f*) if they have the pronoun women commonly use for "I" (*chan*) and the polite word *ka*. Phrases are marked (*m*) if they have "I" for men (*phom*) and the polite word *krup*.

GREETINGS

Hello. (*said by a woman*)
สวัสดีค่ะ
Sa-wat-dee ka.

Hello. (*said by a man*)
สวัสดีครับ
Sa-wat-dee krup.

Where are you going?
ไปไหน
Pai naij?

> I'm going out.
> **ไปเที่ยว**
> Pai thio.

Where have you been?
ไปไหนมา
Pai naij ma?

> I've been to the market.
> **ไปตลาด**
> Pai ta-lat.

Are you well?
สบายดีรึเปล่า
Sa-bai dee reu plao?

Yes, I'm well.
สบายดี
Sa-bai dee.

Thank you. (*f*)   Thank you. (*m*)
ขอบคุณค่ะ   **ขอบคุณครับ**
Kawp-koon ka.   Kawp-koon krup.

It's nothing. / That's OK.
ไม่เป็นไร
Mai pen rai.

Excuse me. (*f*)
ขอโทษค่ะ
Kawj-thot ka.

Excuse me. (*m*)
ขอโทษครับ
Kawj-thot krup.

Good luck.
โชคดี
Chok dee.

Goodbye. (*informal*)
ไปก่อนนะ
Pai gawn, na.

Goodbye. (*polite*)
สวัสดีค่ะ/ครับ
Sa-wat-dee ka/krup.

See you again.
พบกันใหม่
Phop gan mai.

Goodbye. (*formal*)
ลาก่อน
La gawn.

You're invited.
เชิญ
Cheuhn.

Please sit down.
เชิญนั่ง
Cheuhn nang.

Please come in.
เชิญเข้ามา
Cheuhn kao ma.

GENERAL PHRASES

Isn't that right?
ใช่มั้ย

Chai mai?

   Yes, that's right.   No, that's not right.
   ใช่   **ไม่ใช่**

   Chai.   Mai chai.

I'm not sure.
ไม่แน่ใจ

Mai nae-jai.

I don't know.
ไม่รู้

Mai roo.

maybe	certainly	really, truly
บางที	**แน่นอน**	**จริงๆ**
bang-thee	nae-nawn	jing-jing

Is that true?
จริงรึเปล่า
Jing reu plao?

Oh? / Really?
เหรอ

Reuh?

No problem.
ไม่มีปัญหา
Mai mee pan-ha.

whatever (*anything*)
อะไรก็ได้
a-rai gaw dai

wherever (*anywhere*)
ที่ไหนก็ได้
thee-nai gaw dai

whenever (*any time*)
เมื่อไรก็ได้
meua-rai gaw dai

Help!
ช่วยด้วย
Chuay duay!

Calm down.
ใจเย็นๆ
Jai yen-yen.

Wait a minute.
เดี๋ยว / เดี๋ยวๆ
Dioj. / Dioj-dioj.

Be careful.
ระวัง
Ra-wang.

Hurry up.
รีบหน่อย / เร็วๆหน่อย
Reep noi. / Reo-reo noi.

It's up to you.
แล้วแต่คุณ
Laeo tae koon.

Do whatever you like.
ตามสบาย
Tam sa-bai.

I'm indifferent.

เฉยๆ

Cheuy-cheuy.

I can't do it. (*physically*)

ไม่ไหว

Mai wai.

just right

พอดี

phaw dee

adequate / alright

พอใช้ได้

phaw chai dai

the best / the greatest

เยี่ยม

yiam

That's it. / That's all.

แค่นี้

Kae nee.

MAKING FRIENDS

What's your name? (*m*)
คุณชื่ออะไรครับ
Koon cheu a-rai, krup?

My name is Daeng. (*f*)
ฉันชื่อแดง
Chan cheu Daeng.

Where are you from?
คุณมาจากไหน
Koon ma jak nai?

I'm from Chiang Mai. (*m*)
ผมมาจากเชียงใหม่
Phom ma jak Chiang Mai.

Have you eaten yet?
กินข้าวรึยัง
Gin kao reu yang?

Yes, I've eaten already.   No, not yet.
กินแล้ว   **ยัง**
Gin laeo.   Yang.

Where's your house?
บ้านอยู่ที่ไหน
Ban yoo thee-nai?

It's in Bang Na.
อยู่บางนา
Yoo Bang Na.

May I have your phone number?
ขอเบอร์โทรศัพท์หน่อย
Kaw beuh tho-ra-sap noi.

PERSONAL INFORMATION

Where were you born?
คุณเกิดที่ไหน
Koon geuht thee-nai?

I was born in Chiang Mai. (*f*)
ฉันเกิดที่เชียงใหม่
Chan geuht thee Chiang Mai.

How old are you?
คุณอายุเท่าไหร่
Koon a-yoo thao-rai?

I'm 20. (*m*)
ผมอายุยี่สิบ
Phom a-yoo yee-sip.

Are you married? / Do you have a girlfriend/
boyfriend?
คุณมีแฟนหรือยัง
Koon mee faen reu yang?

Yes, I do. (*have-already*)
มีแล้ว
Mee laeo.

No. (*not yet*)
ยัง
Yang.

PASSPORT / CARDS

business card	นามบัตร [nam-bat]
credit card	บัตรเครดิต [bat kray-dit]
driver's license	ใบขับขี่ [bai kap kee]
I.D. card	บัตรประจำตัว [bat pra-jam tua]
immigration office	กองตรวจคนเข้าเมือง [gawng truat kon kao meuang]
passport	พาสปอร์ต [phat-sa-pawt]
visa	วีซ่า [wee-sa]

May I use this card?
ใช้บัตรนี้ได้มั้ย
Chai bat nee dai mai?

I have to extend my visa. (f)
ฉันต้องต่อวีซ่า
Chan tawng taw wee-sa.

May I have your card?
ขอนามบัตรหน่อย
Kawj nam-bat noi.

LANGUAGES

The common pronoun for "she" or "he" is *kao*. "He" and "she" are used interchangably in phrases here.

Thai   ภาษาไทย [pha-saj Thai]

Chinese ภาษาจีน [pha-saj Jeen]

English ภาษาอังกฤษ [pha-saj Ang-grit]

French ภาษาฝรั่งเศส [pha-saj Fa-rang-set]

German ภาษาเยอรมัน [pha-saj Yeuh-ra-mun]

Can you speak English?
คุณพูดภาษาอังกฤษได้มั้ย
Koon phoot pha-saj Ang-grit dai mai?

> Yes. / No.
> **ได้ / ไม่ได้**
> Dai. / Mai dai.

Can you speak Thai?
คุณพูดภาษาไทยได้มั้ย
Koon phoot pha-saj Thai dai mai?

> Just a little.
> **ได้นิดหน่อย**
> Dai nit noi.

> I can't speak Thai. (*m*)
> **ผมพูดภาษาไทยไม่ได้**
> Phomj phoot pha-saj Thai mai dai.

She/He can speak Thai.
เขาพูดภาษาไทยได้
Kao phoot pha-saj Thai dai.

Is there someone who can speak English?

มีใครพูดภาษาอังกฤษได้บ้าง

Mee krai phoot pha-saj Ang-grit dai bang?

Can you teach me Thai? (*m*)

คุณสอนภาษาไทยให้ผมได้มั้ย

Koon sawnj pha-saj Thai hai phomj dai mai?

What does this say? (*reading something*)

นี่อ่านว่าอะไร

Nee an wa a-rai?

It says "welcome".

อ่านว่า "ยินดีต้อนรับ"

An wa "yin dee tawn rap".

UNDERSTANDING / SAYING

Do you understand?
คุณเข้าใจมั้ย
Koon kao-jai mai?

Yes, I understand.
เข้าใจ
Kao-jai.

I don't understand.
ไม่เข้าใจ
Mai kao-jai.

What?
อะไรนะ
A-rai, na?

What did you say?
คุณพูดว่าอะไรนะ
Koon phoot wa a-rai, na?

Please speak slowly.
พูดช้าๆหน่อย
Phoot cha-cha noi.

Please say that again. (can you?)
ช่วยพูดอีกครั้งหนึ่งได้มั้ย
Chuay phoot eeg krang neung, dai mai?

What does "pla" mean?
"ปลา" หมายความว่าอะไร
"Pla" mai-kwam wa a-rai?

It means "fish."
หมายความว่า "fish"
Mai-kwam wa "fish".

What's this called in Thai?
ภาษาไทยเรียกว่าอะไร
Pha-sa Thai riak wa a-rai?

It's called a "broom."
เรียกว่า "ไม้กวาด"
Riak wa "mai gwat".

QUESTION WORDS

WHAT?

Note: Some of the questions in this section end with *bang* (with a falling tone, meaning "some"). It's included when the question might have more than one answer, to make it sound less demanding.

what อะไร [a-rai]

What's this?
นี่คืออะไร
Nee (keu) a-rai?

> This is a map.
> **นี่คือแผนที่**
> Nee keu phaeng-thee.

What are you doing?
ทำอะไร
Tham a-rai?

> I'm studying Thai. (*f*)
> **ฉันเรียนภาษาไทย**
> Chan rian pha-sang Thai.

What are you doing today?
วันนี้คุณจะทำอะไรบ้าง
Wan-nee koon ja tham a-rai bang?

> I'm going to see Wat Pho. (*m*)
> **ผมจะไปเที่ยววัดโพธิ์**
> Phong ja pai thio Wat Pho.

What shall we do?
ทำอะไรดี
Tham a-rai dee?

Let's go to a movie.
ไปดูหนังกันเถอะ
Pai doo <u>nang</u>ɉ gan <u>theuh</u>.

What did you buy?
คุณซื้ออะไรบ้าง
Koon seu a-rai bang?

I bought a book. (*m*)
ผมซื้อหนังสือ
<u>Phom</u>ɉ seu <u>nang</u>ɉ-seuɉ.

I didn't buy anything.
ไม่ได้ซื้ออะไร
Mai dai seu a-rai.

What did she say?
เขาพูดว่าอะไร
Kao phoot wa a-rai?

She said she wasn't coming.
เขาพูดว่าเขาไม่มา
Kao phoot wa kao mai ma.

What's wrong?
เป็นอะไร
Pen a-rai?

I have a headache. (*f*)   Nothing.
ฉันปวดหัว   **ไม่มีอะไร**
Chan <u>puat</u> <u>hua</u>ɉ.   Mai mee a-rai.

WHICH?

For "which" put *nai* after the classifier for the object you're referring to. In Thai, all objects have classifiers that are used in various phrases to refer to the object. There is also a general classifier, *un*, which may be used to refer to any object.

which   ไหน [(*classifier*) naij]

general classifier for things อัน [un]

classifier for buildings   หลัง [langj]

Which one?	Which one do you want?
อันไหน	เอาอันไหน
Un naij?	Ao un naij?

> I want this one.
> เอาอันนี้
> Ao un nee.

Which building?	Which building do you stay in?
หลังไหน	คุณอยู่หลังไหน
Langj naij?	Koon yoo langj naij?

> In that building.
> อยู่หลังนั้น
> Yoo langj nan.

WHAT KIND?

There are four words for "kind," "type," or "style." Two are informal (*yang* and *baep*) and the other two are more formal (*cha-nit* and *pra-phayt*). Two of the words are used for smaller units of things, such as kinds of food, while the other two are for larger units, such as models of houses. *Baep* also means "style" to refer to clothing.

kind (*smaller units*)   ย่าง, ชนิด [yang, cha-nit]

kind, type (*larger units*)   แบบ, ประเภท
[baep, pra-phayt]

what kind   อย่างไหน [yang naij]

what type/style   แบบไหน [baep naij]

What kind do you want? (*kinds of food, etc*)
เอาอย่างไหน
Ao yang naij?

> I want this kind.
> เอาอย่างนี้
> Ao yang nee.

What style of suit do you want?
เอาชุดแบบไหน
Ao choot baep naij?

> I want this style.
> เอาแบบนี้
> Ao baep nee.

I want this style of shirt.
เอาเสื้อแบบนี้
Ao seua baep nee.

WHO?

who   ใคร [krai]

which person   คนไหน [kon naij]

this person   คนนี้ [kon nee]

that person   คนนั้น [kon nan]

nobody   ไม่มีใคร [mai mee krai]

Who did you come with?

คุณมากับใคร

Koon ma gap krai?

I came with a friend. (*f*)

ฉันมากับเพื่อน

Chan ma gap pheuan.

Who are you going with?

คุณจะไปกับใคร

Koon ja pai gap krai?

I'm going with Lek. (*m*)

ผมจะไปกับเล็ก

Phom ja pai gap Lek.

I'm going alone. (*f*)

ฉันจะไปคนเดียว

Chan ja pai kon dio.

Which person is named John?

คนไหนชื่อจอห์น

Kon nai cheu John?

Did anyone come to see me? (*f*)

มีใครมาหาฉันมั้ย

Mee krai ma haj chan mai?

Two people came to see you.

มีสองคนมาหาคุณ

Mee sawng kon ma haj koon.

Nobody came.

ไม่มีใครมา

Mai mee krai ma.

WHERE?

where	ที่ไหน [thee-naij]
where (*shortened*)	ไหน [naij]

Where's your house?
บ้านอยู่ที่ไหน
Ban yoo thee-naij?

It's here.
อยู่ที่นี่
Yoo thee-nee.

It's over there.
อยู่ที่นั้น
Yoo thee-nan.

It's way over there.
อยู่ที่โน่น
Yoo thee-noon.

Where are you going?
คุณจะไปไหน
Koon ja pai naij?

I'm going to the hotel. (*f*)
ฉันจะไปโรงแรม
Chan ja pai rong-raem.

I'm not going anywhere.
ไม่ไปไหน
Mai pai naij.

Where did you go last night?
เมื่อคืนนี้คุณไปไหน
Meua-keun-nee koon pai naij?

I didn't go anywhere.
ไม่ได้ไปไหน
Mai dai pai naij.

Where is Dam?
ดำอยู่ที่ไหน
Dam yoo thee-nai?

Where did Daeng go?
แดงไปไหน
Daeng pai nai?

> She went to the bank.
> **เขาไปธนาคาร**
> Kao pai tha-na-kan.

> I don't know where she went. (*f*)
> **ฉันไม่รู้ว่าเขาไปไหน**
> Chan mai roo wa kao pai nai.

Where's the suitcase?
กระเป๋าอยู่ที่ไหน
Gra-pao yoo thee-nai?

> It's in the room.
> **อยู่ในห้อง**
> Yoo nai hawng.

HOW?

how (*informal*) **ยังไง** [yang-ngai]
how (*formal*) **อย่างไร** [yang-rai]

How is this hotel?
โรงแรมนี้เป็นยังไง
Rong-raem nee pen yang-ngai?

> It's good.
> **ดี**
> Dee.

How do you feel?

คุณเป็นยังไง

Koon pen yang-ngai?

> Fine.
>
> **สบายดี**
>
> Sa-bai dee.

How are you going to Pattaya?

คุณจะไปพัทยายังไง

Koon ja pai Phat-tha-ya yang-ngai?

I'm going by air-conditioned bus.

ไปรถทัวร์ / นั่งรถทัวร์ไป

Pai rot-thua. / Nang rot-thua pai.

WHY?

Put *tham-mai* at the end of affirmative questions ("Why are you ...? / Why did you ...?") and at the beginning of negative questions ("Why aren't you .. .? / Why didn't you ...?").

why   **ทำไม** [tham-mai]

because   **เพราะ, เพราะว่า** [phraw, phraw wa]

Why are you going to Had Yai?

คุณจะไปหาดใหญ่ทำไม

Koon ja pai Had Yai tham-mai?

> I'm going for fun.
>
> **ไปเที่ยว**
>
> Pai thio.

Why aren't you going to Songkla?

ทำไมคุณไม่ไปสงขลา

Tham-mai koon mai pai Song-kla?

Because I don't have time.

เพราะว่าไม่มีเวลา

Phraw wa mai mee way-la.

Why didn't you call me? (*m*)

ทำไมคุณไม่ได้โทรมาหาผม

Tham-mai koon mai dai tho ma haj phomj?

I didn't have your phone number.

ไม่มีเบอร์โทรศัพท์

Mai mee beuh tho-ra-sap.

NUMBERS

CARDINAL NUMBERS

1 หนึ่ง [neung]
2 สอง [sawng]
3 สาม [sam]
4 สี่ [see]
5 ห้า [ha]
6 หก [hok]
7 เจ็ด [jet]
8 แปด [paet]
9 เก้า [gao]
10 สิบ [sip]

For numbers in the teens put the unit number after ten. The exception is 11 which is *sip-et*, not *sip-neung*.

11 สิบเอ็ด [sip-et]
12 สิบสอง [sip-sawng]
13 สิบสาม [sip-sam]
14 สิบสี่ [sip-see]
15 สิบห้า [sip-ha]
16 สิบหก [sip-hok]
17 สิบเจ็ด [sip-jet]
18 สสิบแปด [sip-paet]
19 สิบเก้า [sip-gao]

Do the same for numbers in the twenties.

20 ยี่สิบ [yee-sip]

21 ยี่สิบเอ็ด [yee-sip et]

22 ยี่สิบสอง [yee-sip sawngj]

23 ยี่สิบสาม [yee-sip samj]

24 ยี่สิบสี่ [yee-sip see]

25 ยี่สิบห้า [yee-sip ha]

30, 40, 50, and other two-digit numbers have the unit number before *sip*.

30 สามสิบ [samj-sip]

40 สี่สิบ [see-sip]

50 ห้าสิบ [ha-sip]

60 หกสิบ [hok-sip]

70 เจ็ดสิบ [jet-sip]

80 แปดสิบ [paet-sip]

90 เก้าสิบ [gao-sip]

Add the unit number (examples):

35 สามสิบห้า [samj-sip ha]

48 สี่สิบแปด [see-sip paet]

64 หกสิบสี่ [hok-sip see]

75 เจ็ดสิบห้า [jet-sip ha]

hundred	ร้อย [roi]
thousand	พัน [phan]
ten thousand	หมื่น [meun]
hundred thousand	แสน [saenj]
million	ล้าน [lan]
billion	พันล้าน [phan lan]

500	ห้าร้อย [ha roi]
750	เจ็ดร้อยห้าสิบ [jet roi ha-sip]
1,500	หนึ่งพันห้าร้อย [neung phan ha roi]
	shortened form พันห้า [phan ha]
2,000	สองพัน [sawng phan]
3,000	สามพัน [sam phan]
10,000	หนึ่งหมื่น [neung meun]
20,000	สองหมื่น [sawng meun]
35,000	สามหมื่นห้าพัน [sam meun ha phan]
	shortened form สามหมื่นห้า [sam meun ha]
400,000	สี่แสน [see saen]
5,000,000	ห้าล้าน [ha lan]

ORDINAL NUMBERS AND DATES

Put *thee* (with a falling tone) before cardinal numbers to make ordinal numbers, used in dates and for things in series.

first, number one	ที่หนึ่ง [thee neung]
second, number two	ที่สอง [thee sawng]
the second person	คนที่สอง [kon thee sawng]
date	วันที่ [wan thee]

What date?
วันที่เท่าไหร่
Wan thee thao-rai?

   the first
   วันที่หนึ่ง
   wan thee neung

the first of August
วันที่หนึ่งเดือนสิงหา
wan thee neung deuan Singj-haj

What date are you coming?
คุณจะมาวันที่เท่าไหร่
Koon ja ma wan thee thao-rai?

I'm coming on the 10th.
มาวันที่สิบ
Ma wan thee sip.

"The first" when referring to things in a series
is *raek*, not *thee neung*.

the first day (*ie. of a trip*) วันแรก [wan raek]

the first time   ครั้งแรก [krang raek]

HOW MUCH?

How much?
เท่าไหร่
[thao-rai]

How much money do you have?
คุณมีเงินเท่าไหร่
Koon mee ngeuhn thao-rai?

I have five thousand baht. (*m*)
ผมมีเงินห้าพันบาท
Phomj mee ngeuhn ha phan baht.

How much money did you give him/her?
คุณให้เงินเขาเท่าไหร่
Koon hai ngeuhn kao thao-rai?

I gave him/her a thousand baht. (*f*)

ฉันให้เขาหนึ่งพันบาท

Chan hai kao neung phan baht.

HOW MANY?

Use classifiers to refer to numbers of objects. The classifier for people is *kon*, which in this case is the same as the noun "person/people." "How many people" is *gee kon* and "two people" is *sawng kon*.

How many?

กี่

[gee (*classifier*)]

How many people are going?

ไปกี่คน

Pai gee kon?

Four people are going.

ไปสี่คน

Pai see kon.

How many days are you going for?

ไปกี่วัน

Pai gee wan?

I'm going for three days.

ไปสามวัน

Pai sam wan.

TIME

WHAT TIME?

The system used for telling time in Thai is complicated. The day is divided into four 6-hour periods and each has its own word for "hour" or "o'clock" with 1 AM, 7 AM, 1 PM, and 7 PM all called "one." Officially a 24-hour clock is used with the word *na-lee-ga* for "o'clock." Some times can be expressed in two ways.

6 AM	หกโมงเช้า	[hok mong chao]
7 AM	เจ็ดโมงเช้า	[jet mong chao]
8 AM	แปดโมงเช้า / สองโมงเช้า	[paet mong chao / sawng mong chao]
9 AM	เก้าโมงเช้า / สามโมงเช้า	[gao mong chao / sam mong chao]
10 AM	สิบโมงเช้า / สี่โมงเช้า	[sip mong chao / see mong chao]
11 AM	สิบเอ็ดโมงเช้า / ห้าโมงเช้า	[sip-et mong chao / ha mong chao]
noon	เที่ยง	[thiang]
1 PM	บ่ายโมง	[bai mong]
2 PM	บ่ายสอง	[bai sawng]
3 PM	บ่ายสาม	[bai sam]
4 PM	บ่ายสี่	[bai see]
5 PM	ห้าโมงเย็น	[ha mong yen]
6 PM	หกโมงเย็น	[hok mong yen]
7 PM	หนึ่งทุ่ม	[neung thoom]
8 PM	สองทุ่ม	[sawng thoom]
9 PM	สามทุ่ม	[sam thoom]
10 PM	สี่ทุ่ม	[see thoom]
11 PM	ห้าทุ่ม	[ha thoom]

midnight **เที่ยงคืน** [thiang keun]

1 AM　**ตีหนึ่ง** [tee neung]

2 AM　**ตีสอง** [tee sawng]

3 AM　**ตีสาม** [tee sam]

4 AM　**ตีสี่** [tee see]

5 AM　**ตีห้า** [tee ha]

Add *kreung* for "half past." For minutes say the number followed by *na-thee*. *Tawn* can be included before any time phrase.

What time is it?
กี่โมง / กี่โมงแล้ว
Gee mong? / Gee mong laeo?

> It's 10:30 AM.
> ## สิบโมงครึ่ง
> Sip mong kreung.

What time are you going home?
คุณจะกลับบ้านกี่โมง
Koon ja glap ban gee mong?

> I'm going home at 5:15 PM. (*f*)
> ## ฉันจะกลับบ้านตอนห้าโมงสิบห้านาที
> Chan ja glap ban tawn ha mong sip-ha
> na-thee.

WHEN?

Days/Weeks

Monday　　　**วันจันทร์** [wan Jan]

Tuesday　　　**วันอังคาร** [wan Ang-kan]

Wednesday　　**วันพุธ** [wan Phoot]

Thursday	วันพฤหัส [wan Pha-reu-hat]
Friday	วันศุกร์ [wan Sook]
Saturday	วันเสาร์ [wan Sao]
Sunday	วันอาทิตย์ [wan A-thit]
weekend	เสาร์อาทิตย์ [sao a-thit]
weekday	วันธรรมดา [wan tham-ma-da]
this Monday	วันจันทร์นี้ [wan Jan nee]
next Monday	วันจันทร์หน้า [wan Jan na]
last Monday	วันจันทร์ที่แล้ว
	[wan Jan thee laeo]

Ja is usually included before verbs for sentences in the future but it's optional and can be omitted. Without *ja* the same sentence can be interpreted as past, present, or future with the meaning understood in the context of the conversation.

when	เมื่อไหร่ [meua-rai]
what day	วันไหน [wan nai]

When are you going to Lopburi?
คุณจะไปลพบุรีเมื่อไหร่
Koon ja pai Lop-boo-ree meua-rai?

I'm going to Lopburi on Friday. (*m*)
ผมจะไปลพบุรีวันศุกร์
Phom ja pai Lop-boo-ree wan Sook.

What day did he/she go to Khon Kaen?
เขาไปขอนแก่นวันไหน
Kao pai Kawn Gaen wan nai?

He/She went last Sunday.
เขาไปวันอาทิตย์ที่แล้ว
Kao pai wan A-thit thee laeo.

today	วันนี้ [wan-nee]
yesterday	เมื่อวานนี้ [meua-wan-nee]
tomorrow	พรุ่งนี้ [phroong-nee]
minute	นาที [na-thee]
hour	ชั่วโมง [chua-mong]
day	วัน [wan]
week	อาทิตย์ [a-thit]
month	เดือน [deuan]
year	ปี [pee]
this week	อาทิตย์นี้ [a-thit nee]
next month	เดือนหน้า [deuan na]
last week	อาทิตย์ที่แล้ว [a-thit thee laeo]
last year	ปีที่แล้ว [pee thee laeo]
a moment ago	เมื่อกี้นี้ [meua-gee-nee]
five days ago	ห้าวันที่แล้ว [ha wan thee laeo]
four years ago	สี่ปีที่แล้ว [see pee thee laeo]
in three days	อีกสามวัน [eeg sam wan]
in two weeks	อีกสองอาทิตย์ [eeg sawng a-thit]

When is your friend coming?
เพื่อนจะมาเมื่อไหร่
Pheuan ja ma meua-rai?

My friend is coming next week.
เพื่อนจะมาอาทิตย์หน้า
Pheuan ja ma a-thit na.

When did you come?
คุณมาเมื่อไร
Koon ma meua-rai?

I came two days ago. (*m*)
ผมมาสองวันที่แล้ว
Phom̯ ma sawng̯ wan thee laeo.

When is the bus leaving?
รถจะออกเมื่อไหร่
Rot ja awk meua-rai?

It's leaving in ten minutes.
อีกสิบนาทีจะออก
Eeg sip na-thee ja awk.

OTHER TIME PHRASES

after   หลังจาก [lang̯-jak]

after that   หลังจากนั้น [lang̯-jak nan]

afternoon (*1-4 pm*)   ตอนบ่าย [tawn bai]

afternoon (*5-7 pm*)   ตอนเย็น [tawn yen]

all day   ทั้งวัน [thang wan]

all night   ทั้งคืน [thang keun]

always   ตลอด, เสมอ [ta-lawt, sa-meuh̯]

before (*doing something else*)   ก่อน [gawn]

before (*in the past*)   เมื่อก่อน [meua-gawn]

from … to …   ตั้งแต่ … ถึง [tang-tae … theung̯ …]

in past times   สมัยก่อน [sa-mai̯ gawn]

just   เพิ่ง [pheung (*verb*)]

last night   เมื่อคืนนี้ [meua-keun-nee]

morning   ตอนเช้า [tawn chao]

now   ตอนนี้ [tawn-nee]

now (*right now*)   เดี๋ยวนี้ [dio̯-nee]

since   ตั้งแต่ [tang-tae]

soon   เร็วๆนี้ [reo-reo nee]

then (*at that time*)   ตอนนั้น [tawn-nan]

this afternoon (*early*) ตอนบ่ายนี้ [tawn bai nee]; (*late*) ตอนเย็นนี้ [tawn yen nee]

this morning ตอนเช้านี้ [tawn chao nee]

tonight คืนนี้ [keun-nee]

until ถึง, จนกระทั่ง [theung, jon gra-thang]

when ("~ I went") ตอน, เมื่อ [tawn, meua]

Ann's in Australia now.
ตอนนี้แอนอยู่ออสเตรเลีย
Tawn-nee Ann yoo Aws-tray-lia.

We're going right now.
เราจะไปเดี๋ยวนี้แล้ว
Rao ja pai dioj-nee leuy.

I went to Wat Phra Keo this morning. (*m*)
ตอนเช้านี้ผมไปวัดพระแก้ว
Tawn chao nee phomj pai Wat Phra Gaeo.

I'm going to a party tonight. (*m*)
คืนนี้ผมจะไปงานปาร์ตี้
Keun-nee phomj ja pai ngan pa-tee.

I'm going shopping this afternoon. (*f*)
ตอนบ่ายนี้ฉันจะไปซื้อของ
Tawn bai nee chan ja pai seu kawngj.

After that I'm going to the embassy. (*f*)
หลังจากนั้นฉันจะไปสถานทูต
Langj-jak nan chan ja pai sa-thanj-thoot.

I went to Sukothai before coming here. (*m*)
ผมไปสุโขทัยก่อนมาที่นี่
Phomj pai Soo-koj-thai gawn ma thee-nee.

I was a teacher before. (*f*)

เมื่อก่อนฉันเป็นครู

Meua-<u>gawn</u> chan pen kroo.

I've been here since Friday. (*m*)

ผมอยู่ที่นี่ตั้งแต่วันศุกร์

Phom_j <u>yoo</u> thee-nee tang-<u>tae</u> wan <u>Sook</u>.

She just came.

เขาเพิ่งมา

Kao pheung ma.

When I went to Chiang Mai I visited Doi
    Suthep. (*f*)

ตอนฉันไปเชียงใหม่, ฉันไปเที่ยวดอยสุเทพ

Tawn chan pai Chiang <u>Mai</u>, chan pai thio Doi
    <u>Soo</u>-thayp.

I couldn't sleep all night. (*f*)

ฉันนอนไม่หลับทั้งคืน

Chan nawn mai <u>lap</u> thang keun.

I want to stay here always. (*m*)

ผมยังอยู่ที่นี่ตลอด

Phom_j <u>yak</u> <u>yoo</u> thee-nee ta-<u>lawt</u>.

HOW LONG?

Questions with "how long" are usually phrased
by asking how many days, weeks, etc. someone
has done an activity. *Laeo* is included for
"already." These questions can also be phrased
as "Have you (been doing something) long?"
with the person's response giving the amount of
time he/she has done the activity.

How many days have you been here?

คุณมากี่วันแล้ว

Koon ma gee wan laeo?

I've been here five days.

อยู่ห้าวันแล้ว

Yoo ha wan laeo.

Have you been in Thailand long?

คุณอยู่เมืองไทยนานหรือยัง

Koon yoo meuang Thai nan reu yang?

Yes, a long time.	No, not a long time.
นาน	**ไม่นาน**
Nan.	Mai nan.

I've been in Thailand one month. (*f*)

ฉันอยู่เมืองไทยหนึ่งเดือนแล้ว

Chan yoo meuang Thai neung deuan laeo.

I'll be here for one more week. (*m*)

ผมจะอยู่อีกหนึ่งอาทิตย์

Phom ja yoo eeg neung a-thit.

HOW MANY TIMES? / HOW OFTEN?

Questions with "how often" are usually phrased as "How many times a week?," "How many times a month?," etc.

time (*occasion*)	**ครั้ง** [krang]
how many times	**กี่ครั้ง** [gee krang]
one time	**หนึ่งครั้ง / ครั้งเดียว**
	[neung krang / krang dio]
two times	**สองครั้ง** [sawng krang]

many times	หลายครั้ง [lai krang]
every day	ทุกวัน [thook wan]
every two months	ทุกสองเดือน
	[thook sawng deuan]
all the time	ตลอดเวลา [ta-lawt way-la]
often	บ่อย [boi]
sometimes	บางที / บางครั้ง
	[bang thee / bang krang]
once in a while	นานๆที [nan nan thee]

How many times have you come to Thailand?
คุณมาประเทศไทยกี่ครั้งแล้ว
Koon ma pra-thet Thai gee krang laeo?

I've been here twice.
มาสองครั้งแล้ว
Ma sawng krang laeo.

How often do you study Thai? (*how many times per week*)
คุณเรียนภาษาไทยอาทิตย์ละกี่ครั้ง
Koon rian pha-sa Thai a-thit la gee krang?

I study Thai three times a week. (*f*)
ฉันเรียนภาษาไทยอาทิตย์ละสามครั้ง
Chan rian pha-sa Thai a-thit la sam krang.

I eat Thai food every day. (*f*)
ฉันกินอาหารไทยทุกวัน
Chan gin a-han Thai thook wan.

I go to Malaysia every three months. (*m*)
ผมไปมาเลเซียทุกสามเดือน
Phom pai Ma-lay-sia thook sam deuan.

He/She comes here often.

เขามาที่นี่บ่อย

Kao ma thee-nee boi.

MONTHS & YEARS

Following are the shortened, informal names of the months. Formally there is an additional syllable at the end of the word. Thailand uses Buddhist Era years which begin 543 years before Christian Era years.

what month	เดือนไหน	[deuan naij]
what year	ปีไหน	[pee naij]

January	เดือนมกรา	[deuan Mok-ga-ra]
February	เดือนกุมภา	[deuan Goom-pha]
March	เดือนมีนา	[deuan Mee-na]
April	เดือนเมษา	[deuan May-saj]
May	เดือนพฤษภา	[deuan Phreut-sa-pha]
June	เดือนมิถุนา	[deuan Mee-thoo-na]
July	เดือนกรกฎา	[deuan Ga-ra-ga-da]
August	เดือนสิงหา	[deuan Singj-haj]
September	เดือนกันยา	[deuan Gan-ya]
October	เดือนตุลา	[deuan Too-la]
November	เดือนพฤศจิกา	[deuan Phreut-sa-ji-ga]
December	เดือนธันวา	[deuan Than-wa]

A.D. (Christian Era)
คริสตศักราช, ค.ศ.
[krit-ta-sak-ga-rat, kaw sawj]

B.E. (Buddhist Era)
พุทธศักราช, พ.ศ.
[phoot-tha-sak-ga-rat, phaw sawj]

What month are you coming back?
คุณจะกลับมาเดือนไหน
Koon ja glap ma deuan naij?

I'm coming back in April. (*f*)

ฉันจะกลับมาเดือนเมษา

Chan ja glap ma deuan May-saj.

What year were you born?

คุณเกิดปีไหน

Koon geuht pee naij?

I was born in 1980 (2518). ("one-eight")

ผมเกิดปีหนึ่งแปด

Phomj geuht pee neung-paet.

APPOINTMENTS

appointment	นัด	[nat]
free	ว่าง	[wang]
invite	ชวน, เชิญ	[chuan, cheuhn]
meet	พบ, เจอ	[phop, jeuh]
not free	ไม่ว่าง	[mai wang]

When are you meeting her/him?
คุณจะพบเขาเมื่อไหร่
Koon ja phop kao meua-rai?

> I'm meeting her/him at noon. (*m*)
> **ผมจะพบเขาตอนเที่ยง**
> Phom ja phop kao tawn thiang.

I have an appointment with him/her tomorrow. (*f*)
ฉันมีนัดกับเขาพรุ่งนี้
Chan mee nat gap kao phroong-nee.

Are you free tonight?
คืนนี้ว่างมั้ย
Keun-nee wang mai?

> I'm not free tonight. (*m*)
> **คืนนี้ผมไม่ว่าง**
> Keun-nee phom mai wang.

When shall we meet?
พบกันเมื่อไหร่ดี
Phop gan meua-rai dee?

> Is tomorrow morning OK?
> **พรุ่งนี้เช้าดีมั้ย**
> Phroong-nee chao dee mai?

She/He invited me to a party. (*f*)

เขาชวนฉันไปกินเลี้ยง

Kao chuan chan pai gin liang.

TELEPHONE

Thais generally use polite language on the phone, especially when speaking with someone they don't know. *Koon* is put before names and *ka* or *krup* is added to every sentence.

telephone	โทรศัพท์	[tho-ra-sap]
mobile/cell phone	มือถือ	[meu theu]
telephone number	เบอร์โทรศัพท์	[beuh tho-ra-sap]
telephone line	สาย	[sai]
call to a place	โทรไป	[tho pai]
call here	โทรมา	[tho ma]
extension	ต่อ	[taw]

May I speak to Lek. (*f*)
ขอสายคุณเล็กค่ะ
Kaw sai koon Lek, ka.

This is Lek. (*m*)
นี่เล็กครับ
Nee Lek, krup.

Just a moment. (*f*)
สักครู่ค่ะ
Sak kroo, ka.

Goodbye. (*m*)
สวัสดีครับ
Sa-wat-dee krup.

Someone called you.
มีคนโทรมาหาคุณ
Mee kon tho ma ha koon.

I'd like to call Vietnam. (*f*)

ขอโทรไปเวียดนามได้มั้ยคะ

Kawɟ tho pai Wiet Nam dai mai, ka?

Extension 25, please. (*m*)

ต่อสองห้าครับ

Taw sawngɟ-ha, krup.

SHOPPING

Ka or *krup* should be included with *thao-rai* ("how much"), as a single word can sound rude.

How much? (*f*)

เท่าไหร่คะ

Thao-rai, ka?

How much? (*m*)

เท่าไหร่ครับ

Thao-rai, krup?

Will you take 100 baht?

ร้อยบาทได้มั้ย

Roi baht dai mai?

Can you reduce the price?

ลดให้หน่อยได้มั้ย

Lot hai noi, dai mai?

How much is it altogether?

ทั้งหมดเท่าไหร่

Thang-mot thao-rai?

I haven't received my change.

ยังไม่ได้เงินทอน

Yang mai dai ngeuhn thawn.

May I have a receipt?

ขอใบเสร็จหน่อย

Kaw bai-set noi.

Un in the following sentences is the general classifier used to refer to any object.

How much is this?

อันนี้เท่าไหร่

Un nee thao-rai?

How much is it for two?
สองอันเท่าไหร่
Sawngj un thao-rai?

Do you want this one? (f)
เอาอันนี้มั้ยคะ
Ao un nee mai, ka?

How many do you want?
เอากี่อัน
Ao <u>gee</u> un?

I want one.
เอาหนึ่งอัน / เอาอันหนึ่ง / เอาอันเดียว
Ao <u>neung</u> un. / Ao un <u>neung</u>. / Ao un dio.

I want two.
เอาสองอัน
Ao <u>sawngj</u> un.

May I exchange this? (f)
ขอเปลี่ยนอันนี้ได้มั้ยคะ
<u>Kawj</u> <u>plian</u> un nee dai mai, ka?

Kuat ("bottle") is the classifier for things in bottles.

Do you have drinking water?
มีน้ำเปล่ามั้ย
Mee nam-<u>plao</u> mai?

How much is a bottle?
ขวดละเท่าไหร่
<u>Kuat</u> la thao-<u>rai</u>?

A bottle is ten baht.
ขวดละสิบบาท
<u>Kuat</u> la <u>sip</u> baht.

CLOTHING

clothes, clothing เสื้อผ้า [seua pha]

bathing suit (*men's*) กางเกงว่ายน้ำ [gang-gayng wai nam]; (*women's*) ชุดว่ายน้ำ [choot wai-nam]

belt เข็มขัด [kem kut]

coat เสื้อกันหนาว [seua gan nao]

hat หมวก [muak]

jacket เสื้อกันหนาว [seua gan nao]

jeans กางเกงยีนส์ [gang-gayng yeen]

purse กระเป๋า [gra-pao]

sarong โสร่ง [sa-rong]

shirt เสื้อ [seua]

T-shirt เสื้อยืด [seua yeut]

shoes รองเท้า [rawng-thao]

shorts กางเกงขาสั้น [gang-gayng ka sun]

skirt กระโปรง [gra-prong]

socks ถุงเท้า [thoong thao]

suit ชุด [choot]

sunglasses แว่นกันแดด [waen gan daet]

sweater เสื้อกันหนาว [seua gan nao]

underwear กางเกงใน [gang-gayng nai]

classifier for pieces of clothing ตัว [tua]

classifier for shoes, socks คู่ [koo]

How much is this shirt?

เสื้อตัวนี้เท่าไหร่

Seua tua nee thao-rai?

This shirt is 200 baht.
เสื้อตัวนี้สองร้อยบาท
Seua tua nee sawng roi baht.

May I try it on? (*f*)
ลองใส่ได้มั้ยคะ
Lawng sai dai mai, ka?

Does it fit?
ใส่ได้มั้ย
Sai dai mai?

It fits.	It doesn't fit.
ใส่ได้	ใส่ไม่ได้
Sai dai.	Sai mai dai.

This shirt is nice.
เสื้อตัวนี้สวย
Seua tua nee suay.

Do you like this pair?
ชอบคู่นี้มั้ย
Chawp koo nee mai?

MADE OF

brass	ทองเหลือง	[thawng leuang]
copper	ทองแดง	[thawng daeng]
cotton	ผ้าฝ้าย	[pha fai]
gold	ทอง	[thawng]
iron	เหล็ก	[lek]
ivory	งา, งาช้าง	[nga, nga chang]
jade	หยก	[yok]
leather	หนัง	[nang]

metal   โลหะ [lo-ha]

plastic   พลาสติก [plas-tik]

silk   ผ้าไหม [pha mai]

silver   เงิน [ngeuhn]

steel   เหล็กกล้า [lek gla]

teak   ไม้สัก [mai sak]

What's this made of?
นี่ทำด้วยอะไร
Nee tham duay a-rai?

    It's made of gold.
    ทำด้วยทอง
    Tham duay thawng.

This is a fake.
นี่เป็นของปลอม
Nee pen kawng plawm.

JEWELRY

jewelry   เครื่องประดับ [kreuang pra-dap]

bracelet   สร้อยข้อมือ [soi kaw meu]

    กำไล [gam-lai]

diamond   เพชร [phet]

earrings   ตุ้มหู [toom hoo]

emerald   มรกต [maw-ra-got]

gemstone   พลอย [phloi]

necklace   สร้อย [soi]

    สร้อยคอ [soi kaw]

ring   แหวน [waen]

ruby   ทับทิม [thup-thim]

sapphire   นิล [nín]; (blue) ไพลิน [phai-lín]

classifier for gemstones   เม็ด [met]
classifier for rings   วง [wong]

How much is this gemstone?
เม็ดนี้เท่าไหร่
Met nee thao-rai?

How much is this ring?
วงนี้เท่าไหร่
Wong nee thao-rai?

ORDERING FOOD

barbecued	ย่าง [yang]
breakfast	อาหารเช้า [a-hanɟ chao]
curry soup	แกง [gaeng]
dessert	ของหวาน [kawnɟ wanɟ / ka-nomɟ]
dinner	อาหารเย็น [a-hanɟ yen]
food	อาหาร [a-hanɟ]
fried	(deep-fried) ทอด [thawt]
	(stir-fried) ผัด [phat]
lunch	อาหารกลางวัน [a-hanɟ glang wan]
may I have …	ขอ … [kawɟ …]
minced meat	ลาบ [lap]
not fully cooked	ไม่สุก [mai sook]
not spicy	ไม่เผ็ด [mai phet]
order food	สั่งอาหาร [sang a-hanɟ]
raw	ดิบ [dip]
ripe	สุก [sook]
roasted	อบ [op]
salad (spicy)	ยำ [yam]
seafood	อาหารทะเล [a-hanɟ tha-lay]
snack (n)	ขนม [ka-nomɟ]
soup (boiled)	ต้ม [tom]
steamed	นึ่ง [neung]
sweet and sour	เปรี้ยวหวาน [prio-wanɟ]
to go (in a bag)	ใส่ถุง [sai thoongɟ]
unripe	ไม่สุก [mai sook]
vegetarian	เจ [jay]; (eat as) กินเจ [gin jay]
vegetarian food	อาหารเจ [a-hanɟ jay]
with (lit. "put")	ใส่ [sai]

without (*lit.* "don't put") ไม่ใส่ [mai sai]

without chili pepper ไม่ใส่พริก [mai sai phrik]

without meat ไม่ใส่เนื้อ [mai sai neua]

without milk ไม่ใส่นม [mai sai nom]

without MSG ไม่ใส่ผงชูรส [mai sai phong
choo rot]

without sugar ไม่ใส่น้ำตาล [mai sai nam-tan]

May I have a menu?
ขอเมนูด้วย
Kawɟ may-noo duay.

May I have a menu in English?
ขอเมนูภาษาอังกฤษ
Kawɟ may-noo pha-saɟ Ang-grit.

I'd like iced coffee to go.
ขอกาแฟเย็นใส่ถุง
Kawɟ ga-fae yen sai thoongɟ.

I didn't order this.
อันนี้ไม่ได้สั่ง
Un nee mai dai sang

Waiter! / Waitress!
น้อง
Nawng!

Check please. (*in a cheap restaurant*)
เก็บตังค์ด้วย
Gep-tang duay.

Check please. (*in an expensive restaurant*)
เช็คบิลด้วย
Chek-bin duay.

Keep the change.

ไม่ต้องทอน

Mai tawng thawn.

Order food by numbers of plates, bowls, glasses, bottles, etc.

bottle	**ขวด** [kuat]
bottle	(*large*) **ขวดใหญ่** [kuat yai]
	(*small*) **ขวดเล็ก** [kuat lek]
bowl	(*large*) **ชาม** [cham]
	(*small*) **ถ้วย** [thuay]
chopsticks	**ตะเกียบ** [ta-giap]
cup	**ถ้วย** [thuay]
fork	**ส้อม** [sawm]
glass	**แก้ว** [gaeo]
knife	**มีด** [meet]
plate	**จาน** [jan]
spoon	**ช้อน** [chawn]
straw	**หลอด** [lawt]

I'd like one plate of fried rice with chicken.

ขอข้าวผัดไก่หนึ่งจาน

Kawj kao-phat gai neung jan.

I'd like one bottle of drinking water.

ขอน้ำเปล่าหนึ่งขวด

Kawj nam-plao neung kuat.

I'd like two glasses of water.

ขอน้ำเปล่าสองแก้ว

Kawj nam-plao sawngj gaeo.

How much is a bottle of beer?
เบียร์ขวดเท่าไหร่
Bia kuat la thao-rai?

DRINKS เครื่องดื่ม [kreuang deum]

beer	**เบียร์**	[bia]
	(*draft*) **เบียร์สด**	[bia sot]
coffee	(*hot*) **กาแฟร้อน**	[ga-fae rawn]
	(*iced*) **กาแฟเย็น**	[ga-fae yen]
ice	**น้ำแข็ง**	[nam kaeng]
lemonade	**น้ำมะนาว**	[nam ma-nao]
liquor	**เหล้า**	[lao]
milk	**นม**	[nom]
orange drink	**น้ำส้ม**	[nam som]
orange juice (fresh)	**น้ำส้มคั้น**	[nam som kun]
rice wine	**เหล้าขาว**	[lao kao]
smoothie (banana)	**กล้วยปั่น**	[gluay pun]
soda water	**น้ำโซดา**	[nam so-da]
tea	**น้ำชา**	[nam-cha]
tea (Chinese)	**น้ำชาจีน**	[nam-cha jeen]
water (drinking)	**น้ำเปล่า**	[nam plao]
wine	**เหล้าไวน์**	[lao wai]

THAI FOOD

condiments	**เครื่องปรุง**	[kreuang proong]
basil	**ใบโหระพา**	[bai ho-ra-pha]
basil (spicy)	**กะเพรา**	[ga-phrao]
chili sauce	**น้ำพริก**	[nam phrik]
coconut milk	**น้ำกะทิ**	[nam ga-thee]
coriander leaf	**ผักชี**	[phak chee]

curry paste	น้ำพริก [nam phrik]
curry powder	ผงกะหรี่ [phong ga-ree]
fermented fish	ปลาร้า [pla-ra]
	ปลาแดก [pla-daek]
fish sauce	น้ำปลา [nam pla]
galangal	ข่า [ka]
garlic	กระเทียม [gra-thiam]
garnishes	เครื่องปรุง [kreuang proong]
ginger	ขิง [king]
honey	น้ำผึ้ง [nam pheung]
MSG	ผงชูรส [phong choo rot]
onions	หอมใหญ่ [hawm yai]
oyster sauce	น้ำมันหอย [nam-mun hoi]
pepper	(*black*) พริกไท [phrik thai]
	(*chili*) พริก [phrik]
	(*small, hot*) พริกขี้หนู
	[phrik kee noo]
salt	เกลือ [gleua]
soy sauce	ซีอิ๊ว [see iu]
sugar	น้ำตาล [nam-tan]

VEGETABLES	ผัก [phak]
bamboo shoots	หน่อไม้ [naw-mai]
beans (green)	ถั่วฝักยาว [thua fuk yao]
cabbage	กะหล่ำ [ga-lum]
cashew nuts	เม็ดมะม่วง [met ma-muang]
cauliflower	กะหล่ำดอก [ga-lum dawk]
corn	ข้าวโพด [kao-phot]
baby corn	ข้าวโพดอ่อน [kao-phot awn]
cucumber	แตงกวา [taeng gwa]

eggplant	(*long*) มะเขือยาว [ma-keuaɟ yao]
	(*small*) มะเขือ [ma-keuaɟ]
lettuce	ผักกาด [phak-gat]
morning glory	ผักบุ้ง [phak boong]
greens (large)	ผักคะน้า [phak ka-na]
mushrooms	เห็ด [het]
pea pods	ถั่วลันเตา [thua lun tao]
peanuts	ถั่ว [thua]
potatoes	มันฝรั่ง [mun fa-rang]
squash	ฟัก [fuk]
tofu	เต้าหู้ [tao-hoo]
tomatoes	มะเขือเทศ [ma-keuaɟ-thet]
MEAT	เนื้อ [neua]
beef	เนื้อ [neua]
	เนื้อวัว [neua wua]
chicken	ไก่ [gai]
duck	เป็ด [pet]
eggs	ไข่ [kai]
fish	ปลา [pla]
frog	กบ [gop]
innards	เครื่องใน [kreuang nai]
liver	ตับ [tap]
meatballs	ลูกชิ้น [look chin]
pork	หมู [mooɟ]
	(*pickled*) แหนม [naemɟ]
pork bologna	หมูยอ [mooɟ yaw]
wild boar	หมูป่า [mooɟ pa]
sausage	ไส้กรอก [sai grawk]
water buffalo	เนื้อควาย [neua kwai]

FISH ปลา [pla]

catfish ปลาดุก [pla dook]

crab ปู [poo]

shellfish หอย [hoi]

shrimp กุ้ง [goong]

squid ปลาหมึก [pla meuk]

RICE ข้าว [kao]

white rice (steamed) ข้าวเปล่า [kao plao]

sticky rice ข้าวเหนียว [kao nio]

brown rice ข้าวกล้อง [kao glawng]

rice soup ข้าวต้ม [kao tom]

NOODLES ก๋วยเตี๋ยว [guay-tio]

large white noodles เส้นใหญ่ [sen yai]

small white noodles เส้นเล็ก [sen lek]

yellow noodles บะหมี่ [ba-mee]

FOLLOWING ARE EXAMPLES OF THAI FOOD:

barbecued chicken
ไก่ย่าง [gai yang]

curry, hot red with beef
แกงเผ็ดเนื้อ [gaeng phet neua]

curry, green with chicken
แกงเขียวหวานไก่ [gaeng kio-wan gai]

fried chicken
ไก่ทอด [gai thawt]

fried pork with garlic
หมูทอดกระเทียม [moo thawt gra-thiam]

fried rice with chicken
ข้าวผัดไก่ [kao-phat gai]

minced chicken, spicy
ลาบไก่ [lap gai]

omelet with pork and vegetables
ไข่ยัดไส้ [kai yat-sai]

papaya salad
ส้มตำ [som-tam]

roast chicken
ไก่อบ [gai op]

salad, spicy with squid
ยำปลาหมึก [yam pla meuk]

soup, mildly seasoned
ต้มจืด [tom jeut]

soup, spicy with seafood
ต้มยำทะเล [tom yam tha-lay]

steamed crab
ปูนึ่ง [poo neung]

stir-fried beef with spicy basil
เนื้อผัดกะเพรา [neua phat ga-phrao]

stir-fried catfish with curry paste
ปลาดุกผัดเผ็ด [pla dook phat phet]

stir-fried chicken with ginger
ไก่ผัดขิง [gai phat king]

stir-fried mixed vegetables
ผัดผักรวมมิตร [phat phak ruam mit]

stir-fried morning glory
ผัดผักบุ้ง [phat phak boong]

sweet and sour shrimp
กุ้งผัดเปรี้ยวหวาน [goong phat prio-wan]

tempura
ชุปแป้งทอด [choop paeng thawt]

vegetarian *phak kana*
ผักคะน้าเจ [phak ka-na jay]

WESTERN FOOD

bread	ขนมปัง [ka-nom pang]
butter	เนย [neuy]
cheese	เนยแข็ง [neuy kaeng]
french fries	มันฝรั่งทอด [mun fa-rang thawt]
fried egg	ไข่ทอด [kai dao]
ham	หมูแฮม [moo haem]
jam	แยม [yaem]
omelet	ไข่เจียว [kai jio]
toast	ขนมปังปิ้ง [ka-nom pang ping]
vegetable salad	สลัดผัก [sa-lat phak]

FRUIT	ผลไม้ [phon-la-mai]
banana	กล้วย [gluay]
coconut	มะพร้าว [ma-phrao]
durian	ทุเรียน [thoo-rian]
grapes	องุ่น [a-ngoon]
guava	ฝรั่ง [fa-rang]
jackfruit	ขนุน [ka-noon]
lime	มะนาว [ma-nao]
longan	ลำไย [lum-yai]
lychee	ลิ้นจี่ [lin-jee]
mango	มะม่วง [ma-muang]
mangosteen	มังคุด [mang-koot]
papaya	มะละกอ [ma-la-gaw]

pineapple	สับปะรด [sap-pa-rot]
rambutan	เงาะ [ngaw]
sugar cane	อ้อย [oi]
tamarind	มะขาม [ma-kamɲ]
tangerine	ส้ม [som]
watermelon	แตงโม [taeng mo]

Food in a produce market is bought by weight or by the piece.

How much is a kilo? (*f*)
โลเท่าไหร่คะ
Lo thao-rai, ka?

A kilo is 40 baht.
โลละสี่สิบบาท
Lo la see-sip baht.

I'd like one kilo.
เอากิโลหนึ่ง
Ao gee-lo neung.

I'd like two kilos.
เอาสองกิโล
Ao sawngɲ gee-lo.

How much is this piece of fruit?
ลูกนี้เท่าไหร่
Look nee thao-rai?

I'd like this one.
เอาลูกนี้
Ao look nee.

PEOPLE & FAMILY

person, people	คน [kon]
adult	ผู้ใหญ่ [phoo yai]
baby	(up to 2 years) เด็กอ่อน [dek awn]
	(2 to 5 years) เด็กเล็ก [dek lek]
child, children	(in general) เด็ก [dek]
	(of your own) ลูก [look]
boy	เด็กผู้ชาย [dek phoo-chai]
girl	เด็กผู้หญิง [dek phoo-ying]
man	ผู้ชาย [phoo-chai]
young man	หนุ่ม [noom]
woman	ผู้หญิง [phoo-ying]
young woman	สาว [sao]

FAMILY ครอบครัว [krawp-krua]

relative(s)	ญาติ [yat]
mother	แม่ [mae]
father	พ่อ [phaw]
parents	พ่อแม่ [phaw-mae]
sister	(older) พี่สาว [phee-sao]
	(younger) น้องสาว [nawng-sao]
brother	(older) พี่ชาย [phee-chai]
	(younger) น้องชาย [nawng-chai]
brothers and sisters	พี่น้อง [phee-nawng]
wife	แฟน [faen] / เมีย [mia] / ภรรยา [phan-ra-ya]
husband	แฟน [faen] / สามี [sa-mee]

child, children	(*of your own*) ลูก [look]
daughter	ลูกสาว [look-saoɟ]
son	ลูกชาย [look-chai]

grandmother	(*maternal*) ยาย [yai]
	(*paternal*) ย่า [ya]
grandfather	(*maternal*) ตา [ta]
	(*paternal*) ปู่ [poo]
grandchild	หลาน [lanɟ]

aunt (*older sister of mother or father*)
ป้า [pa]

uncle (*older brother of mother or father*)
ลุง [loong]

aunt / uncle (*younger on mother's side*)
น้า [na]

aunt / uncle (*younger on father's side*)
อา [ah]

niece, nephew	หลาน [lanɟ]
cousin	ลูกพี่ลูกน้อง
	[look-phee-look-nawng]

How many children do you have?
คุณมีลูกกี่คน
Koon mee look gee kon?

I have two children. (*f*)
ฉันมีลูกสองคน
Chan mee look sawngɟ kon.

I don't have any children.
ไม่มีลูก
Mai mee look.

This is my older brother.

คนนี้เป็นพี่ชาย

Kon nee pen phee-chai.

COUNTRIES & NATIONALITIES

foreign country ต่างประเทศ [tang pra-thet]

foreigner คนต่างประเทศ [kon tang pra-thet]

hilltribe person ชาวเขา [chao kao]

Indian or Muslim (*person*) แขก [kaek]

Africa	อัฟริกา [A-free-ga]	
Asia	เอเชีย [Ay-sia]	
Europe	ยุโรป [Yoo-rop]	
Middle East	ตะวันออกกลาง [Ta-wan awk glang]	

America	อเมริกา [A-may-ree-ga]
	สหรัฐ [Sa-ha-rat]
Australia	ออสเตรเลีย [Aws-tray-lia]
Bali	บาหลี [Ba-lee]
Cambodia	เขมร [Ka-men]
	กัมพูชา [Gum-phoo-cha]
Canada	แคนาดา [Kae-na-da]
China	เมืองจีน [Meuang Jeen]
England	ประเทศอังกฤษ [Pra-thet Ang-grit]
France	ฝรั่งเศส [Fa-rang-set]
Germany	เยอรมัน [Yeuh-ra-mun]
Hong Kong	ฮ่องกง [Hawng Gong]
India	อินเดีย [In-dia]
Indonesia	อินโดนีเซีย [In-do-nee-sia]
Italy	อิตาลี [It-ta-lee]
Japan	ญี่ปุ่น [Yee-poon]
Korea	เกาหลี [Gao-lee]

Laos	ประเทศลาว [Pra-thet Lao]
	เมืองลาว [Meuang Lao]
Malaysia	มาเลเซีย [Ma-lay-sia]
Myanmar	พม่า [Pha-ma]
Philippines	ฟิลิปปินส์ [Fee-lip-peen]
Russia	รัสเซีย [Rat-sia]
Saudi Arabia	ซาอุ [Sa-oo]
Singapore	สิงคโปร์ [Sing-ka-po]
Switzerland	สวิส [Sa-wit]
Vietnam	เวียดนาม [Wiet Nam]

Use the name of the country to make adjectives like "German" and "French."

Have you ever eaten Italian food?
คุณเคยกินอาหารอิตาลีมั้ย
Koon keuy gin a-han It-ta-lee mai?

Kon is put before the name of a country to refer to people of that nationality. *Chao* (meaning "inhabitant of") is also used in some phrases. *Meuang* and *pra-thet* both mean "country," and *meuang* also means "city."

American (*person/people*)
คนอเมริกา [kon A-may-ree-ga]

Asian (*person/people*)
ชาวเอเชีย [chao Ay-sia]

European (*person/people*)
ชาวยุโรป [chao Yoo-rop]

Thai (*person/people*)
คนไทย [kon Thai]

Westerner **ฝรั่ง** [fa-rang]

JOBS & BUSINESS

JOBS

actor, actress	นักแสดง [nak sa-daeng]
airplane pilot	นักบิน [nak bin]
ambassador	ทูต [thoot]
architect	สถาปนิก [sa-thaɰ-pa-nik]
artist	ช่างวาดรูป [chang wat roop]
assistant	ผู้ช่วย [phoo chuay]
athlete	นักกีฬา [nak gee-la]
barber	ช่างตัดผม [chang tat phomɰ]
boss (*n*)	หัวหน้า [huaɰ na]
businessman/ woman	นักธุรกิจ [nak thoo-ra-git]
construction worker	ช่างก่อสร้าง [chang gaw sang]
cook (*n*)	คนครัว [kon krua]
	(*female*) แม่ครัว [mae krua]
	(*male*) พ่อครัว [phaw krua]
dentist	หมอฟัน [mawɰ fun]
doctor	หมอ [mawɰ]
driver	คนขับรถ [kon kap rot]
electrician	ช่างไฟฟ้า [chang fai-fa]
employee	ลูกจ้าง [look jang]
engineer	วิศวกร [weet-sa-wa-gawn]
farmer	ชาวนา [chao na]
fisherman	คนหาปลา [kon haɰ pla]
fortune-teller	หมอดู [mawɰ doo]
government worker	ข้าราชการ [ka-rat-cha-gan]
guard (watchman)	ยาม [yam]
guide	ไกด์ [gai]
housewife	แม่บ้าน [mae ban]

laborer	กรรมกร [gam-ma-gawn]
lawyer	ทนาย [tha-nai]
	ทนายความ [tha-nai kwam]
manager	ผู้จัดการ [phoo jat-gan]
masseur/masseuse	หมอนวด [maw nuat]
mechanic	ช่างซ่อมรถ [chang sawm rot]
model	(*female*) นางแบบ [nang baep]
	(*male*) นายแบบ [nai baep]
musician	นักดนตรี [nak don-tree]
nurse	พยาบาล [pha-ya-ban]
	นางพยาบาล [nang pha-ya-ban]
police officer	ตำรวจ [tam-ruat]
politician	นักการเมือง [nak gan meuang]
professor	อาจารย์ [a-jan]
prostitute	โสเภณี [soj-phay-nee]
	(*vulgar term*) กะหรี่ [ga-lee]
psychiatrist	จิตแพทย์ [jit-ta-phaet]
reporter	นักข่าว [nak kao]
scientist	นักวิทยาศาสตร์ [nak wit-tha-ya-sat]
secretary	เลขา [lay-kaj]
seller	(*female*) แม่ค้า [mae ka]
	(*male*) พ่อค้า [phaw ka]
servant	คนใช้ [kon chai]
singer	นักร้อง [nak rawng]
soldier	ทหาร [tha-hanj]
staff, staffperson	พนักงาน [pha-nak-ngan]
student	นักเรียน [nak rian]
teacher	ครู [kroo]
tourist	นักท่องเที่ยว [nak thawng thio]

translator   ล่าม [lam]
ผู้แปล [phoo phlae]

What work do you do?
คุณทำงานอะไร
Koon tham-ngan a-rai?

> I'm a dentist. (*f*)
> ฉันเป็นหมอฟัน
> Chan pen maw fun.

Where do you work?
คุณทำงานที่ไหน
Koon tham-ngan thee-nai?

> I work in Lard Phrao. (*m*)
> ผมทำงานที่ลาดพร้าว
> Phom tham-ngan thee Lat Phrao.

Do you have a day off?
มีวันหยุดมั้ย
Mee wan yoot mai?

> I'm off on Sunday.
> หยุดวันอาทิตย์
> Yoot wan A-thit.

BUSINESS

business (do ~)   ทำธุรกิจ [tham thoo-ra-git]
capital (*investment*) ทุน [thoon]
     เงินทุน [ngeuhn thoon]
company (*business*) บริษัท [baw-ree-sat]
export   ส่งออก [song awk]
factory   โรงงาน [rong-ngan]

go bankrupt	ล้มละลาย [lom-la-lai]
goods	สินค้า [sin-ka]
import	นำเข้า [nam kao]
invest	ลงทุน [long thoon]
lose money (in business)	ขาดทุน [kat thoon]
manufacture	ผลิต [pha-lit]
office	ออฟฟิต [awf-fit]
profit (n)	กำไร [gam-rai]
retail	ขายปลีก [kai pleek]
stock	หุ้น [hoon]
stock market	ตลาดหุ้น [ta-lat hoon]
wholesale	ขายส่ง [kai song]

They invested in this company.
พวกเขาลงทุนในบริษัทนี้
Phuak kao long thoon nai baw-ree-sat nee.

The stock market is going up.
ตลาดหุ้นขึ้น
Ta-lat hoon keun.

The stock market is going down.
ตลาดหุ้นลง
Ta-lat hoon long.

This company imports goods from Japan.
บริษัทนี้นำสินค้าเข้าจากประเทศญี่ปุ่น
Baw-ree-sat nee nam sin-ka kao jak pra-thet
Yee-poon.

This company exports rice.
บริษัทนี้ส่งออกข้าว
Baw-ree-sat nee song awk kao.

This company makes a good profit.

บริษัทนี้ได้กำไรดี

Baw-ree-<u>sat</u> nee dai gam-rai dee.

BANKING

account	บัญชี [ban-chee]
ATM card	บัตรเอทีเอ็ม [bat ATM]
bank	ธนาคาร [tha-na-kan]
banknote, bill	แบงค์ [baeng]
branch (*of a bank*)	สาขา [saj-kaj]
cash (*n*)	เงินสด [ngeuhn sot]
cash a check	ขึ้นเงิน [keun ngeuhn]
change (*small bills*)	แบงค์ย่อย [baeng yoi]
coins	เหรียญ [rianj]
deposit	ฝาก [fak]
dollar	ดอล [dawn]
	ดอลลาร์ [dawn-la]
exchange money	แลกเงิน [laek ngeuhn]
withdraw	เบิก [beuhk]
	ถอน [thawnj]

I'd like to exchange money.
ขอแลกเงินหน่อย
Kawj laek ngeuhn noi.

Do you have change (*small bills*)?
มีแบงค์ย่อยมั้ย
Mee baeng yoi mai?

I'd like to open an account.
ขอเปิดบัญชีหน่อย
Kawj peuht ban-chee noi.

I'd like to cash a check.
ขอขึ้นเงินหน่อย
Kawj keun ngeuhn noi.

BANKING

I'd like to withdraw some money.

ขอเบิกเงินหน่อย

<u>Kaw</u>ɟ <u>beu</u>hk ngeuhn <u>no</u>i.

POST OFFICE

letter	จดหมาย	[jot-mai]
post office	ไปรษณีย์	[prai-sa-nee]
package, parcel	พัสดุ	[phat-sa-doo]
register	ลงทะเบียน	[long tha-bian]
stamp	แสตมป์	[sa-taem]

Send this to America. (*m*)
ส่งอันนี้ไปอเมริกาครับ
Song un nee pai A-may-ree-ga, krup.

I'd like to register it.
ขอลงทะเบียนด้วย
Kaw long tha-bian duay.

PARTS OF THE BODY

body	ตัว [tua]
abdomen	ท้อง [thawng]
arm	แขน [kaeng]
back	หลัง [lang]
beard	เครา [krao]
blood	เลือด [leuat]
blood vessel	เส้นเลือด [sen leuat]
bone	กระดูก [gra-dook]
brain	สมอง [sa-mawng]
breasts	นม [nom]
buttocks	ก้น [gon]
chest	อก [ok]
ear	หู [hoo]
eye	ตา [ta]
face	หน้า [na]
finger	นิ้ว [niu]
fingernail	เล็บมือ [lep meu]
foot	เท้า [thao]
hair	(on the body) ขน [kon]
	(on the head) ผม [phom]
hand	มือ [meu]
head	หัว [hua]
heart	หัวใจ [hua-jai]
kidney	ไต [tai]
knee	หัวเข่า [hua kao]
leg	ขา [ka]
lips	ริมฝีปาก [rim fee pak]
liver	ตับ [tap]

lungs	ปอด [pawt]
moustache	หนวด [nuat]
mouth	ปาก [pak]
muscle	กล้าม [glam]
neck	คอ [kaw]
nerves	ประสาท [pra-sat]
nose	จมูก [ja-mook]
skin	ผิว [phiɯ]
stomach	กระเพาะ [gra-phaw]
	ท้อง [thawng]
throat	คอ [kaw]
tongue	ลิ้น [lin]
tooth	ฟัน [fun]
waist	เอว [eo]

MEDICAL

medicine	ยา [ya]
medicine (*traditional*)	ยาแผนโบราณ [ya phaeŋ bo-ran]
medicine to relieve …	ยาแก้ … [ya gae …]

abscess	ฝี [feeŋ]
AIDS	โรคเอดส์ [rok ayt]
allergic to …	แพ้ … [phae …]
ambulance	รถพยาบาล [rot pha-ya-ban]
backache	ปวดหลัง [puat langŋ]
band-aid	พลาสเตอร์ [plas-teuh]
blood test	ตรวจเลือด [truat leuat]
broken leg	ขาหัก [kaŋ hak]
cancer	มะเร็ง [ma-reng]
cut (finger, etc)	บาด [bat]
dengue fever	ไข้เลือดออก [kai leuat awk]
disease	โรค [rok]
dizzy	เวียนหัว [wian huaŋ]
doctor	หมอ [mawŋ]
faint	เป็นลม [pen lom]
food poisoning	อาหารเป็นพิษ [a-hanŋ pen phit]
flu	ไข้หวัดใหญ่ [kai wat yai]
give birth	ออกลูก [awk look]
	คลอดลูก [klawt look]
hospital	โรงพยาบาล [rong-pha-ya-ban]
hurt	(*adj*) (*injured*) บาดเจ็บ [bat jep]
	(*v*) (*it hurts*) เจ็บ [jep]
infected	อักเสบ [ak-sayp]
injection	ฉีดยา [cheet ya]

itches	คัน [kun]
malaria	มาลาเลีย [ma-la-ria]
numb	ชา [cha]
operate	ผ่าตัด [pha tat]
pill, capsule	เม็ด [met]
sore throat	เจ็บคอ [jep kaw]
swollen	บวม [buam]
tetanus	บาดทะยัก [bat-tha-yak]
typhoid fever	ไทฟอยด์ [thai-foi]
unconscious	สลบ [sa-lop]
	หมดสติ [mot sa-tee]
vomit	อวก [uak]
	อาเจียน [a-jian]
weak	อ่อนแอ [awn ae]
worms (*intestinal*)	พยาธิ [pha-yat]
wound	แผล [phlae]

Please call a doctor.
ช่วยเรียกหมอด้วย
Chuay riak maw duay.

a doctor who speaks English
หมอที่พูดภาษาอังกฤษได้
maw thee phoot pha-sa Ang-grit dai

I want to go to the hospital. (*f*)
ฉันอยากไปโรงพยาบาล
Chan yak pai rong-pha-ya-ban.

Where's the hospital? (*m*)
โรงพยาบาลอยู่ที่ไหนครับ
Rong-pha-ya-ban yoo thee-nai, krup?

Please call an ambulance.
ช่วยเรียกรถพยาบาลด้วย

Chuay riak rot pha-ya-ban duay.

I'm not well. (*f*)
ฉันไม่สบาย

Chan mai sa-bai.

I'm ill. (*f*)
ฉันป่วย

Chan puay.

I have a fever. (*f*)
ฉันเป็นไข้

Chan pen kai.

I have a cold. (*f*)
ฉันเป็นหวัด

Chan pen wat.

I have a cough. (*f*)
ฉันไอ

Chan ai.

I have a headache. (*m*)
ผมปวดหัว

Phom puat hua.

I have a stomachache. (*m*)
ผมปวดท้อง

Phom puat thawng.

I have diarrhea. (*m*)
ผมท้องเสีย

Phom thawng sia.

I have no strength.
ไม่มีแรง
Mai mee raeng.

Do you have cough medicine?
มียาแก้ไอมั้ย
Mee ya gae ai mai?

Take this medicine.
กินยานี้
Gin ya nee.

How many should I take?
กินกี่เม็ด
Gin gee met?

> Take two.
> กินสองเม็ด
> Gin sawng met.

How many times a day?
วันละกี่ครั้ง
Wan la gee krang?

> Three times a day.
> วันละสามครั้ง
> Wan la sam krang.

PLACES IN TOWN

bank	ธนาคาร [tha-na-kan]
barber shop	ร้านตัดผม [ran tat phom]
beauty shop	ร้านเสริมสวย [ran seuhm suay]
bookstore	ร้านขายหนังสือ [ran kai nang-seu]
bridge	สะพาน [sa-phan]
canal	คลอง [klawng]
drugstore	ร้านขายยา [ran kai ya]
embassy	สถานทูต [sa-than-thoot]
expressway	ทางด่วน [thang duan]
fountain	น้ำพุ [nam phoo]
gas station	ปั้มน้ำมัน [pum nam-mun]
hotel	โรงแรม [rong-raem]
intersection	(3-way) สามแยก [sam yaek]
	(4-way) สี่แยก [see yaek]
market	ตลาด [ta-lat]
	(produce) ตลาดสด [ta-lat sot]
movie theater	โรงหนัง [rong-nang]
museum	พิพิธภัณฑ์ [phee-phit-tha-phan]
park	สวน [suan]
police station	สถานีตำรวจ [sa-tha-nee tam-ruat]
post office	ไปรษณีย์ [prai-sa-nee]
road	ถนน [tha-non]
school	โรงเรียน [rong-rian]
street	ถนน [tha-non]
	(side street, lane) ซอย [soi]
swimming pool	สระว่ายน้ำ [sa wai-nam]
restaurant	ร้านอาหาร [ran-a-han]
shopping center	ศูนย์การค้า [soon gan-ka]

| tailor | ร้านตัดเสื้อ [ran tat seua] |
| traffic circle | วงเวียน [wong-wian] |

ASKING DIRECTIONS

When asking strangers for directions add *ka* (for women) or *krup* (for men) to be polite.

across from	ตรงข้าม	[trong kam]
around here	แถวนี้	[thaeo nee]
before a place	ก่อนถึง	[gawn theung]
behind	ข้างหลัง	[kang lang]
beneath	ข้างล่าง	[kang lang]
between … and …	ระหว่าง … กับ …	[ra-wang … gap …]
beyond a place (*past a place*)	เลย	[leuy]
downstairs	ข้างล่าง	[kang lang]
facing	ข้างหน้า	[kang na]
far	ไกล	[glai]
in, inside	ใน	[nai]
	ข้างใน	[kang nai]
in front of	ข้างหน้า	[kang na]
near (to)	ใกล้	[glai]
	ใกล้ๆ	[glai-glai]
next to	ข้างๆ	[kang-kang]
	ติดกับ	[tit (gap)]
on top of	ข้างบน	[kang bon]
outside	ข้างนอก	[kang nawk]
past (*beyond a place*)	เลย	[leuy]
straight, go straight	ตรงไป	[trong pai]
turn left	เลี้ยวซ้าย	[lio sai]
turn right	เลี้ยวขวา	[lio kwa]
upstairs	ข้างบน	[kang bon]

Where's the hospital? (*m*)
โรงพยาบาลอยู่ที่ไหนครับ
Rong-pha-ya-ban <u>yoo</u> <u>thee-naij</u>, <u>krup</u>?

It's over there.
อยู่ที่โน่น
<u>Yoo</u> <u>thee-noon</u>.

Which side is it on?
อยู่ข้างไหน
<u>Yoo</u> <u>kang naij</u>?

It's on the right.
อยู่ข้างขวา
<u>Yoo</u> <u>kang kwaj</u>.

It's on the left.
อยู่ข้างซ้าย
<u>Yoo</u> <u>kang sai</u>.

Which way should I go?
ไปทางไหน
<u>Pai</u> thang <u>naij</u>?

Go this way.
ไปทางนี้
<u>Pai</u> thang <u>nee</u>.

What street is it on?
อยู่ถนนอะไร
<u>Yoo</u> tha-<u>nonj</u> a-<u>rai</u>?

It's on Sukhumvit Rd.
อยู่ถนนสุขุมวิท
<u>Yoo</u> tha-<u>nonj</u> <u>Soo-koomj</u>-wit.

What floor is it on?
อยู่ชั้นไหน
<u>Yoo</u> chan <u>naij</u>?

It's on the third floor.
อยู่ชั้นสาม
Yoo chan samɟ.

Is it far?
ไกลมั้ย
Glai mai?

Yes. / It's far.	No. / It's not far.
ไกล	ไม่ไกล
Glai.	Mai glai.

The bank is next to the hotel.
ธนาคารอยู่ข้างๆโรงแรม
Tha-na-kan yoo kang-kang rong-raem.

The restaurant is before the intersection.
ร้านอาหารอยู่ก่อนถึงสี่แยก
Ran-a-hanɟ yoo gawn theungɟ see-yaek.

The movie theater is in the shopping center.
โรงหนังอยู่ข้างในศูนย์การค้า
Rong-nangɟ yoo kang nai soonɟ gan ka.

DRIVING INSTRUCTIONS

Please go to Sanam Luang. (*m*)

ไปสนามหลวงครับ

Pai Sa-_nam_ _Luang_, krup

Go in this side street.

เข้าซอยนี้เลย

Kao soi nee leuy.

Go a little further.

ไปอีกหน่อย

Pai _eeg_ _noi_.

Stop here.

จอดที่นี่

Jawt thee-nee.

Could you drive slowly? (*f*)

ขับช้าๆหน่อย ได้มั้ยคะ

Kap cha-cha _noi_, dai mai, ka?

There's a traffic jam.

รถติด

Rot tit.

TRAVEL & TRANSPORTATION

Note that the general word for vehicles, here written *rot*, is pronounced "rote," or sometimes "lote" in colloquial Thai.

ROAD TRAVEL

bicycle	จักรยาน	[jak-gra-yan]
car	รถยนต์	[rot-yon]
motorcycle	มอเตอร์ไซด์	[maw-teuh-sai]
~ helmet	หมวกกันน็อก	[muak gan nawk]

pick-up with benches
สองแถว [sawng-thaeo]

vehicle (*general term*) รถ [rot]
classifier for vehicles คัน [kun]

Do you have motorcycles for rent?
มีมอเตอร์ไซด์ให้เช่ามั้ย
Mee maw-teuh-sai hai chao mai?

How much is it for one day?
วันละเท่าไหร่
Wan la thao-rai?

TAXI

taxi แท็กซี่ [thaek-see]
   three-wheeled (*motorized*)
   ตุ๊กตุ๊ก [took-took]
   three-wheeled (*pedal, samlor*)
   สามล้อ [sam-law]

How much is it to Silom? (*taxi*)
ไปสีลมเท่าไหร่
Pai See-lom thao-rai?

You have to be at the airport at 7 AM.
ต้องอยู่สนามบินตอนเจ็ดโมงเช้า
Tawng yoo sa-nam bin tawn jet mong chao.

AIR TRAVEL

airplane	เครื่องบิน	[kreuang bin]
airport	สนามบิน	[sa-nam bin]

TRAIN TRAVEL

train	รถไฟ	[rot-fai]
train station	สถานีรถไฟ	[sa-tha-nee rot-fai]

ticket **ตั๋ว** [tua]

one-way	เที่ยวเดียว	[thio dio]
round trip	ไปกลับ	[pai glap]
first class	ชั้นหนึ่ง	[chan neung]
second class	ชั้นสอง	[chan sawng]
third class	ชั้นสาม	[chan sam]
classifier for tickets ใบ	[bai]	

sleeping compartment **ตู้นอน** [too nawn]

What time is the train to Surat Thani?
รถไฟไปสุราษฎร์ธานีกี่โมง
Rot-fai pai Soo-rat Tha-nee gee mong?

I'd like one ticket to Phetburi.
ขอตั๋วไปเพชรบุรีหนึ่งใบ
Kaw tua pai Phet-boo-ree neung bai.

BUS TRAVEL

bus
   (*within city*) **รถเมล์** [rot-may]
   (*city-to-city*) **รถธรรมดา** [rot tham-ma-da]
   (*city-to-city, air-conditioned*) **รถทัวร์** [rot thua]

arrive (at a place)	ไปถึง	[pai theung]
bus route	สาย	[sai]
bus station	คิวรถ	[kiu rot]
bus stop	ป้ายรถเมล์	[pai rot-may]
leave (a place)	ออก	[awk]

Is there a bus to Sukothai?
มีรถไปสุโขทัยมั้ย
Mee rot pai Soo-koj-thai mai?

Which bus?
คันไหน
Kun nai?

> This bus.
> **คันนี้**
> Kun nee.

What time is the bus to Mae Sot?
รถไปแม่สอดออกกี่โมง
Rot pai Mae Sawt awk gee mong?

> A bus leaves at 8 AM.
> **รถออกแปดโมงเช้า**
> Rot awk paet mong chao.

> A bus leaves every hour.
> **มีรถออกทุกชั่วโมง**
> Mee rot awk thook chua-mong.

What time will we arrive?
ไปถึงกี่โมง
Pai theung gee mong?

> It arrives at 6 PM.
> **ไปถึงตอนหกโมงเย็น**
> Pai theung tawn hok mong yen.

How long does it take to get to Pattaya?
ไปพัทยาใช้เวลาเท่าไหร่
Pai Phat-tha-ya chai way-la thao-rai?

It takes about two hours.
ใช้เวลาประมาณสองชั่วโมง
Chai way-la pra-man sawng chua-mong.

How far is it to Chiang Saen?
ไปเชียงแสนกี่กิโล
Pai Chiang Saen gee gee-lo?

It's about fifty kilometers.
ประมาณห้าสิบกิโล
Pra-man ha-sip gee-lo.

BOAT TRAVEL

boat   **เรือ** [reua]
pier   **ท่าเรือ** [tha reua]

classifier for boats   **ลำ** [lum]

Is there a boat to Ko Tao?
มีเรือไปเกาะเต่ามั้ย
Mee reua pai Gaw Tao mai?

That boat goes to Ko Tao.
ลำนั้นไปเกาะเต่า
Lum nan pai Gaw Tao.

AT HOTEL

bed	(*double*) **เตียงเดี่ยว** [tiang dio]
	(*single, paired*) **เตียงคู่** [tiang koo]
hotel	**โรงแรม** [rong-raem]
key	**กุญแจ** [goon-jae]
room	**ห้อง** [hawng]
	(*air conditioned*) **ห้องแอร์** [hawng ae]
	(*regular*) **ห้องธรรมดา** [hawng tham-ma-da]

Do you have a room? (*m*)
มีห้องมั้ยครับ
Mee hawng mai, krup?

How much is a room? (*f*)
ห้องเท่าไหร่คะ
Hawng thao-rai, ka?

I'd like an air-conditioned room. (*f*)
เอาห้องแอร์คะ
Ao hawng ae, ka.

I'd like a double bed.
เอาเตียงเดี่ยว
Ao tiang dio.

How many nights are you staying?
อยู่กี่คืน
Yoo gee keun?

I'm staying two nights.
อยู่สองคืน
Yoo sawng keun.

May I have the key?

ขอกุญแจด้วย

Kaw goon-jae duay.

What's your room number?

ห้องเบอร์อะไร

Hawng beuh a-rai?

HOUSE & RENTALS

apartment	อพาร์ทเม้นต์ [a-phat-men]
bathroom	ห้องน้ำ [hawng nam]
bed	เตียง [tiang]
bedroom	ห้องนอน [hawng nawn]
bedsheet	ผ้าปูที่นอน [pha poo thee-nawn]
blanket	ผ้าห่ม [pha hom]
broom	ไม้กวาด [mai gwat]
bucket	ถัง [thang]
cabinet	ตู้ [too]
chair	เก้าอี้ [gao-ee]
curtains	ผ้าม่าน [pha man]
cushion	เบาะ [baw]
door	ประตู [pra-too]
floor	พื้น [pheun]
for rent	ให้เช่า [hai chao]
frying pan	กระทะ [gra-tha]
furniture	เฟอร์นิเจอร์ [feuh-nee-jeuh]
garage	โรงรถ [rong rot]
hanger	ไม้แขวนเสื้อ [mai kwaeng seua]
house, home	บ้าน [ban]
iron	เตารีด [tao reet]
kitchen	ห้องครัว [hawng krua]
lamp	โคมไฟ [kom fai]
landlord, landlady	เจ้าของบ้าน [jao kawng ban]
lightbulb	หลอดไฟ [lawt fai]
mat	เสื่อ [seua]
mattress	ที่นอน [thee-nawn]
mirror	กระจก [gra-jok]

oven	เตาอบ [tao op]
pillow	หมอน [mawng]
pillowcase	ปลอกหมอน [plawk mawng]
pot	หม้อ [maw]
refrigerator	ตู้เย็น [too yen]
roof	หลังคา [langj-ka]
room	ห้อง [hawng]
shower fixture	ฝักบัว [fuk bua]
stairs	บันได [bun-dai]
stove	เตาอบ [tao op]
table	โต๊ะ [to]
towel	ผ้าเช็ดตัว [pha chet tua]
wall	(*garden*) กำแพง [gam-phaeng]
	(*inside*) ฝา [faj]
washing machine	เครื่องซักผ้า [kreuang sak pha]
wastebasket	ถังขยะ [thangj ka-ya]
water jar	ตุ่ม [toom]
window	หน้าต่าง [na-tang]
window screen	มุ้งลวด [moong luat]

classifier for buildings หลัง [langj]

I live in this house. (*f*)
ฉันอยู่บ้านหลังนี้
Chan yoo ban langj nee.

I want to rent a house. (*f*)
ฉันอยากจะเช่าบ้าน
Chan yak ja chao ban.

How much is the rent per month?
ค่าเช่าเดือนละเท่าไหร่
Ka chao deuan la thao-rai?

ANIMALS & INSECTS

animal	สัตว์ [sàt]
classifier for animals	ตัว [tua]
wild animal	สัตว์ป่า [sàt pà]
pet	สัตว์เลี้ยง [sàt liang]
female (*animal*)	ตัวเมีย [tua mia]
male (*animal*)	ตัวผู้ [tua phoo]

ant	มด [mót]
bat	ค้างคาว [kang-kao]
bear	หมี [meeɹ]
bee	ผึ้ง [pheung]
bird	นก [nók]
butterfly	ผีเสื้อ [pheeɹ seua]
cat	แมว [maeo]
kitten	ลูกแมว [look maeo]
cockroach	แมลงสาบ [má-laeng sàp]
crocodile	จระเข้ [jaw-rá-kay]
deer	กวาง [gwang]
dog	หมา, สุนัข [maɹ, sŏo-nák]
puppy	ลูกหมา [look maɹ]
elephant	ช้าง [chang]
fly	แมลงวัน [má-laeng wan]
frog	กบ [gòp]
goat	แพะ [phae]
horse	ม้า [ma]
insect	แมลง [má-laeng]
kangaroo	จิงโจ้ [jing-jò]

lizard	(*chameleon*) กิ้งก่า [ging-ga]
	(*large house*) ตุ๊กแก [took-gae]
	(*small house*) จิ้งจก [jing-jok]
monkey	ลิง [ling]
mosquito	ยุง [yoong]
mouse	หนู [nooj]
owl	นกฮูก [nok hook]
rabbit	กระต่าย [gra-tai]
rat	หนู [nooj]
scorpion	แมงป่อง [maeng pawng]
shark	ปลาฉลาม [pla cha-lamj]
sheep	แกะ [gae]
snake	งู [ngoo]
tiger	เสือ [seuaj]
turtle	เต่า [tao]
whale	ปลาวาฬ [pla wan]

How many dogs do you have?
คุณมีหมากี่ตัว
Koon mee maj gee tua?

    I have three.
    มีสามตัว
    Mee samj tua.

GAMES & SPORTS

badminton	แบด [baet]
ball-kicking game	ตะกร้อ [ta-graw]
basketball	บาส [bat]
	บาสเก็ตบอล [bas-get-bawn]
beat (*win*)	ชนะ [cha-na]
boat racing	เครื่องเรือ [kaeng reua]
box (*v*)	ชกมวย [chok muay]
boxing	(*international*) มวยสากล [muay sa-gon]
	(*Thai*) มวยไทย [muay Thai]
bull fighting	(*Thai*) ชนวัว [chon wua]
cards (play ~)	เล่นไพ่ [len phai]
checkers	หมากฮอด [mak hawt]
chess	หมากรุก [mak rook]
chicken fighting	ชนไก่ [chon gai]
fighting fish	ปลากัด [pla gat]
football (soccer)	ฟุตบอล [foot-bawn]
gamble	เล่นการพนัน [len gan pha-nan]
golf	กอล์ฟ [gawp]
golf course	สนามกอล์ฟ [sa-nam gawp]
kite fighting	แข่งว่าว [kaeng wao]
lose (to)	แพ้ [phae]
referee	กรรมการ [gam-ma-gan]
soccer	ฟุตบอล [foot-bawn]
sports	กีฬา [gee-la]
sports field	สนามกีฬา [sa-nam gee-la]
swimming	ว่ายน้ำ [wai-nam]
team	ทีม [theem]

tennis	เทนนิส [then-nit]
tennis court	สนามเทนนิส [sa-nam̩ then-nit]
win	ชนะ [cha-na]

What sports do you like?
คุณชอบกีฬาอะไร
Koon chawp gee-la a-rai?

> I like football (soccer).
> **ชอบฟุตบอล**
> Chawp foot-bawn.

Who won?
ใครชนะ
Krai cha-na?

> Our team won.
> **ทีมของเราชนะ**
> Theem kawng̩ rao cha-na.

The Malaysian team lost.
ทีมมาเลเซียแพ้
Theem Ma-lay-sia phae.

WEATHER

atmosphere	อากาศ [a-gat]
cloud(s)	เมฆ [mayk]
cold	หนาว [nao]
cold season	หน้าหนาว [na nao]
degree (temp)	องศา [ong-sa]
dew	น้ำค้าง [nam kang]
flood	น้ำท่วม [nam thuam]
fog	หมอก [mawk]
hot	ร้อน [rawn]
hot season	หน้าร้อน [na rawn]
lightning	ฟ้าแลบ [fa laep]
rain	ฝน [fon]
rainbow	รุ้ง [roong]
rainy season	หน้าฝน [na fon]
season	หน้า, ฤดู [na, reu-doo]
snow	หิมะ [hee-ma]
storm	พายุ [pha-yoo]
sunshine	แดด [daet]
temperature	อุณหภูมิ [oon-ha-phoom]
thunder	ฟ้าร้อง [fa rawng]
weather	อากาศ [a-gat]
wind (*n*)	ลม [lom]

The weather's good today.
วันนี้อากาศดี
Wan-nee a-gat dee.

It's hot.
อากาศร้อน
A-gat rawn.

It's cool.

อากาศเย็น

A-<u>gat</u> yen.

It's cold.

อากาศหนาว

A-<u>gat</u> <u>nao</u>ı.

What's the temperature?

อุณหภูมิเท่าไหร่

Oon-<u>ha</u>-phoom <u>thao-rai</u>?

   It's 30 degrees.

   สามสิบองศา

   <u>Sam</u>ı-<u>sip</u> ongˍ-<u>sa</u>ı.

It's raining.

ฝนตก

<u>Fon</u>ı <u>tok</u>.

The wind is blowing.

ลมพัด

Lom <u>phat</u>.

The sun is shining.

แดดออก

<u>Daet</u> <u>awk</u>.

IN THAILAND

Bangkok	กรุงเทพฯ [Groong-thayp]
central Thailand	ภาคกลาง [phak glang]
eastern Thailand	ภาคตะวันออก [phak ta-wan awk]
northeastern Thailand	ภาคอีสาน [phak Ee-san]
northern Thailand	ภาคเหนือ [phak neua]
southern Thailand	ภาคใต้ [phak tai]

border	ชายแดน [chai-daen]
city, town	เมือง [meuang]
village	หมู่บ้าน [moo ban]
province	จังหวัด [jang-wat]
district	อำเภอ [am-pheuh]
sub-district	ตำบล [tam-bon]

What province are you from?
คุณมาจากจังหวัดอะไร
Koon ma jak jang-wat a-rai?

I'm from Nong Khai province. (f)
ฉันมาจากจังหวัดหนองคาย
Chan ma jak jang-wat Nawng Kai.

THAI CULTURE

amulet	พระเครื่อง [phra kreuang]
bamboo mouth organ	แคน [kaen]
city pillar shrine	หลักเมือง [lak meuang]
cymbals	ฉิ่ง [ching], ฉาบ [chap]
dance (circle)	รำวง [ram-wong]
dance (masked)	โขน [kon]
flower garland	พวงมาลัย [phuang ma-lai]
giant	ยักษ์ [yak]
Krathong holiday	ลอยกระทง [loi gra-thong]
music (*Isan, Lao*)	หมอลำ [maw lum]
music (*Thai country*)	ลูกทุ่ง [look thoong]
Naga (*serpent*)	นาค [nak]
ogre	ยักษ์ [yak]
opera	(*Central Thai*) ลิเก [lee-gay]
	(*Chinese*) งิ้ว [ngiu]
	(*Southern Thai*) มโนราห์ [ma-no-ra]
shadow puppet play	หนังตะลุง [nang ta-loong]
Singha (lion)	สิงห์ [sing]
spirit house	ศาลพระภูมิ [san-phra-phoom]
string tying ceremony	บายศรีสู่ขวัญ [bai-see soo kwan]
temple fair	งานวัด [ngan wat]
Thai New Year	สงกรานต์ [Song-gran]
Thai orchestra	วงปี่พาทย์ [wong pee-phat]
throw water	รดน้ำ [rot nam]
tying strings on wrists	ผูกขอมือ [phook kaw meu]

RELIGIONS OF THAILAND

religion **ศาสนา** [sat-sà-naɟ]

What's your religion?
คุณนับถือศาสนาอะไร
Koon nap-theuɟ sàt-sà-naɟ a-rai?

> I'm a Buddhist. (*f*)
> **ฉันนับถือศาสนาพุทธ**
> Chan nap-theuɟ sàt-sà-naɟ Phoot.

BUDDHISM

Buddha	**พระพุทธเจ้า** [Phra Phoot-tha-jao]
Buddhism	**ศาสนาพุทธ** [sàt-sà-naɟ Phoot]
Buddhist	**คนนับถือศาสนาพุทธ** [kon nap-theuɟ sàt-sà-naɟ Phoot]
chant	**สวดมนต์** [suat mon]
dharma (teachings)	**ธรรมะ** [tham-ma]
give food to monks	**ทำบุญตักบาตร** [tham boon tak bat]
karma	**กรรม** [gam]
make merit	**ทำบุญ** [tham boon]
meditate	**นั่งสมาธิ** [nang sà-ma-thee]
monk	**พระ** [phra]
monk's quarters	**กุฏิ** [goo-tee]
morning alms round	**บิณฑบาต** [bin tha bat]
novice	**เณร** [nayn]
	สามเณร [samɟ-ma-nayn]
nun	**แม่ชี** [mae chee]
ordain	**บวช** [buat]

ordination party	งานบวชนาค	[ngan buat nak]
Pali (*language*)	บาลี	[Ba-lee]
reclining Buddha	พระนอน	[Phra nawn]
Sanskrit (*language*)	สันสกฤต	[Sun-sa-grit]
statue of Buddha	พระพุทธรูป	[Phra Phoot-tha-roop]
stupa (pagoda)	เจดีย์	[je-dee]
temple building	โบสถ์	[bot]
temple compound	วัด	[wat]

CHRISTIANITY

Bible	พระคัมภีร์	[Phra Kam-phee]
Christian	คนนับถือศาสนาคริสต์	[kon nap-theu sat-sa-na Krit]
Christianity	ศาสนาคริสต์	[sat-sa-na Krit]
Christmas	คริสต์มาส	[Krit-sa-mat]
church	โบสถ์	[bot]
go to church	เข้าโบสถ์	[kao bot]
Jesus	พระเยซู	[Phra Yay-soo]

ISLAM

Allah	พระอัลเลาะห์	[Phra Al-law]
Islam	ศาสนาอิสลาม	[sat-sa-na It-sa-lam]
Koran	อัลกุรอาน	[An Goo-la-an]
Mohammed	มุฮัมมัด	[Mo-ham-mut]
mosque	สุเหร่า, มัสยิด	[soo-rao, mas-yeet]
Muslim	มุสลิม	[Moot-sa-lim]

JUDAISM

Jew	คนนับถือศาสนายิวส์	[kon nap-theu sat-sa-na Yiu]